SECOND SERIES

The Collectors Encyclopedia of

ROSEVILLE POTTERY

By
Sharon and Bob Huxford

COLLECTOR BOOKS
A Division of Schroeder Publishing Co., Inc.

TABLE OF CONTENTS

ABOUT THE AUTHORS

Since writing The Collectors Encyclopedia of Roseville Pottery, Volume I, the Huxfords have been named Pottery Editors for Collector Books, and over the past several years have written several books on the Ohio art potteries — The Collectors Encyclopedias of McCoy, Brush-McCoy and Weller Pottery; and the Collectors Catalogues of Early Roseville and Brush-McCoy. They are also the authors of The Encyclopedia of Fiesta, now in its third edition.

FOREWORD

In the four years since The Collectors Encyclopedia of Roseville Pottery, Volume I was published, new lines, new information, and many fine examples of Roseville's art have been reported to us, and we felt it time to share this exciting knowledge with collectors everywhere. This Volume has been prepared as a companion to the first book — please refer to it for historical information, marks of the pottery (although several newly discovered marks appear among the color plates), and artist's signatures in addition to those listed in Volume II.

We feel confident that you will enjoy seeing some of the best examples of the early art ware ever produced . . . exceptional pieces in the early Blended Glaze . . . and a fine representation of Middle Period lines such as Futura, Imperial and Pinecone, to name but a few. Jardinieres and pedestals and umbrella stands are always popular; several pages are devoted to them . . . and wall pocket collectors will find that more than 140 are shown.

It has been our pleasure to prepare this book for those who love Roseville . . . "beauty that never fades."

Note Hexagon with lid in broken glaze.

SUMMARY IN RETROSPECT,
Art Ware to Commercial Lines

In the early days of the history of the Roseville Pottery Company, distribution of their wares was sometimes accomplished by peddlers who regularly made their rounds, hauling assorted goods from door to door, eking out their sustenance by providing the housewife with everyday necessities and an occasional trinket. Before their main office was moved from Roseville to Zanesville in 1898, the company promoted a package deal — a sampling of their wares — which they referred to in their advertisements as the "Canvaser's Outfit." (The ad copy is printed in part in the color section). From the assorted wares they offered, we can learn a little more concerning the type of pottery they produced prior to the turn of the century. A miniature cuspidor and umbrella stand were offered "finished in blended colors, artistically decorated, represent-(ing) exactly full size ware." (No doubt this blended ware represented a goodly part of their production. Catalogues printed a few years later indicate the retail prices for some of these early blended glazed pieces — the stork umbrella stand, $1.25, some of the mid-price jardinieres and pedestals, $4-$6, and one 45″ tall jard and ped with female heads sold for $15-$20. Although none of this early ware was marked, be aware of the shape numbers: jardinieres carry #s 400-499; pedestals #500-599; cuspidors #600-699; and umbrella stands #700-799). Also in the ad, a miniature cooking crock "too well known to need comment" was listed as #315; the salesman's sample Venetian crock on page 38 was probably one of these. It is marked with a three digit number on the base — the first is a 3; the last two are not clear.

Roseville began the production of art pottery in their Zanesville plant in 1900. The lovely brown glazed Rozane is familiar to all Roseville collectors, and the light Rozane, although by no means as plentiful, is nearly always represented by at least one example in almost any serious collection. There are other variations within the line, however, that are extremely scarce. Two types, shown in the color plates are, by reason of their unique coloring, very rare and exciting! One is done in a monochromatic palette of soft brown. The other has blended background effects that almost exactly duplicate Weller's Aurelian line — gold and orange streaking is deftly worked in with the dark brown to produce a striking backdrop for the vivid, natural hues of the painting. (Rozane shapes are often elaborate, just as often very simple . . . shape #s begin at 800, and run to 999. A small piece of Rozane could be bought for as little as $5; the large floor vases were as high as $90).

In the early years after the turn of the century until as late as 1920, almost any pottery company in the area manufactured a matt green line. Roseville's first green line in 1904 was called Rozane Egypto. In 1907, their Chloron line was introduced and it was followed a few years later with another, called simply Matt Green. Collectors have tried to devise an identification process that would separate unmarked Chloron from Egypto by associating the various glaze characteristics with one particular line. Careful comparison of marked examples shows no distinction, but the catalogue pages reprinted in Volume I and in The Collectors Catalogue of Early Roseville Pottery will often settle the question of line identification.

Rozane Mara, introduced in 1904, was Roseville's answer to the famous Sicardo line by the S. A. Weller Pottery. Today, Mara is much rarer than Sicardo, and is almost never marked. Three variations of the lustre glaze are shown in the color plates — each very distinct. In one, the intricate pattern is in sharp contrast to the red lustre background; in a second, the design is very subtle, and tends to blend into the overall color. The third and most desirable glaze is brilliant magenta with highlighted areas of metallic lustre over a shape modeled in low relief.

One of the most famous of these early art ware lines was Della Robbia. The 1906 Rozane catalogue shows vases, urns, tankards and bowls in sgraffito, decorations colorfully enameled, shapes with dramatic styling and often with reticulated rim designs. Close observation of later catalogues reveals a completely remodeled line. On page 59 of The Collectors Catalogue of Early Roseville Pottery, the Della Robbia shapes are more familiar as Aztec, see page 60. Not one of the 1906 shapes are shown. No handles, no reticulation, less quality and impact in the designs . . . a sign of the onset of mass production.

This may also explain the fact that many pieces of Rozane Crystalis are found on simple Rozane shapes, rather than those futuristic, almost space age shapes shown in the 1906 catalogues. Two schools of thought exist concerning the evaluation of Rozane Crystalis. Collectors of crystaline glazes judge the quality of the crystals within the glaze . . . others prefer the old Crystalis shapes over the more simple Rozane ones.

With little if any information available concerning the early line called Special in the Roseville catalogues, the answers to some of our questions may never be found. Was this ware decorated by Roseville, or were their shapes decorated by another company, and finally sold through Roseville's own catalogues? The lovely tankard on page 30 is signed by Gasper — a known Pickard China Co. decorator.

ROZANE CATALOGUE IN REVIEW

To the collector who has developed a sincere appreciation for the quality of workmanship, the careful attention to detail so apparent in the Roseville product, any type of related material is a coveted treasure — especially such an item as one of the very early Rozane Ware catalogues. Due to the fact that a vast majority of these promotional pamphlets were laid aside, forgotten, and eventually discarded, the number of them that have survived the past 75 years is very small, indeed, and they are considered quite rare. Because many collectors may never have the opportunity to see one of these for themselves, the following articles have been selected from two of these booklets — one is dated 1905.

How Rozane Originated

Many collectors have asked how we came to make Rozane. It was like this:

A certain well-known artist whose special delight was the painting of flowers, sat one evening before a half-finished canvas, intently poring, by the last fading rays of daylight, over a book. At last, sighing, he looked up at his canvas across which reflections of the sunset were cast, mingled with deep shadows.

"Too bad, too bad," said the voice of a stranger, who had been drinking in the charm of the scene.

"You startled me," said the artist, turning, "but listen to this," and he lighted a candle while he read, never thinking to ask who the stranger might be. "It is Ruskin I was reading. Mentioning the permanency of ceramic works as compared with those of other branches of art, he says:

"It is surely a severe lesson to us that the best works of Turner could not be shown for six months without being destroyed. I have hope of one day interesting you greatly in the study of the arts of moulding and painting porcelain; and of turning the attention of the workmen of Italy from the vulgar perishable mosaic to the exquisite subtleties of form and color possible in the perfectly docile and afterward imperishable clay. And one of the ultimate results of such craftsmanship might be the production of pictures as brilliant as painted glass — as delicate as the most subtle water colors, and more permanent than the Pyramids."

"I was only thinking, when you spoke, what a shame it is that these efforts of mine have to go the way of Turner's. I'd like to try my hand at the clay."

It reads like a romance, but just here began the Rozane idea of reproducing in art pottery fine productions in oils. The stranger, it chanced, was a skilled potter, then engaged in making models for our less expensive potteries. He set aside a laboratory for experiments and so successful was he that, with the aid of his new-found collaborator, the artist, the soft and natural tints of nature were not only transmitted to the clay but preserved, practically unaltered, even through the intense firing to which the ware is subjected.

The natural tendencies of the Ohio clays run to golden browns and yellows, and these tones, artistically blended, formed the body and background of the first Rozane and are retained in all designs of this first style, now called Rozane Royal, to distinguish it from the new varieties constantly being designed in our studios.

With permanence in art as the prime motive, the first attempts in Rozane have resulted in the organization of a company of artists attracted by the worthy object which prompted the first experiments. These artists are all earnest students in ceramics and all have ideas of their own which they are anxious to work out. The spirit of experiment always prevails in our studios and laboratories. Moreover, each artist has his or her own style and no design is ever duplicated. This accounts for the wide variety of subjects and the strong individuality found in Rozane.

Holding up an ideal for the perfect pottery, a well-known authority on ceramics says:

"Let us suppose that a piece of pottery has been painted, and that the action of the fire has made the coloring perennial, so that we find in it a design as everlasting as the ware itself. Let us suppose, further, that the tints are natural, that, in short, the design is all that it should be, and that in the painting nature is displayed as on the canvas — then we would have a specimen of the perfect union of the potter's and of the painter's art."

This is ROZANE ROYAL.

THE STORY OF ROZANE
... from the early Rozane Ware Booklet.

Upon the edge of the picturesque city of Zanesville, Ohio, stand the plants of the Roseville Pottery Company where the famous Rozane Ware is conceived and executed.

How Rozane Ware differs from other wares, how it acquires that certain something which makes it a distinctive art creation appealing universally to connoisseurs, can perhaps be best explained by an imaginary "little journey" through the plants.

The logical starting point of such an expedition would be the modeling and designing rooms, where artists, carefully selected for their creative ability, are constantly engaged in the evolution of new and graceful patterns.

In one corner stands the old-time potter's wheel, made famous by story and song, on which the material, under the modeler's skillful touch, gathers grace and takes on the faultless symmetry that must characterize every line of every piece created.

None of the hurly-burly of commercialism invades this sanctum of art. The modeler lingers long and earnestly over each piece, taking his own chosen time, often working for days, and even weeks, on a delicately turned bit of ware.

No pattern leaves this room until it has passed the critical eye of the master-artist, for nothing short of the highest degree of excellence may bear the Rozane mark.

After the pattern is completed a cast of it is made from which subsequent molds are produced. The clay, which comes from the neighboring hills and which is of a particularly desirable quality, is prepared for use by grinding in what is known as a "blunger" mill, after which it is passed through a fine screen, insuring a smooth and equal consistency. Water is added until a slip of the proper thickness is formed, and it is then ready to pour into the molds which reproduce the various patterns.

It is here that a nice bit of skill and judgment is required. The mold is filled entirely with the thin slip, which immediately begins to adhere to the sides of the mold and to harden. The workman, at just the proper moment, empties the mold of the liquid that is in the center, leaving only sufficient adhering to the sides to form the requisite thickness of the vase or whatever the piece may be. The mold is left in a steam-drying room for twenty-four hours; afterward the piece is removed, carefully sponged to insure perfect smoothness, the handle (if handle there be), is attached, and the piece is ready for blending.

The last few steps have been purely mechanical. We are now in the domain of art again. Before being turned over to the blender each piece, at this stage, is subjected to a critical examination. If it shows even the most minute imperfection, back it goes to the grinder — that is the Rozane way.

The blending is done by compressed air brushes. Perhaps in this blending, as much as in any other part of the production, is the individual artistic quality of Rozane Ware attained. It is not a mere spraying of color upon color, but the delicate harmonizing of tints and tones, of velvety shadows and shimmering high-lights — a true conception of coloring by artists who feel and know.

The newly blended pieces are kept in the moist atmosphere of the "damp-room," until their turn comes in the finishing room where they are hand-decorated by painters carefully chosen for skill and intelligence. Whether the decoration be a spray of roses or a sprig of ferns, a collection of poppies or a cluster of autumn leaves, the warmth of coloring and fidelity of execution prove the splendid efficiency of the staff of decorators. Many of these decorators are graduates of the great European art schools; others are from the most efficient American institutions — thus embracing the best foreign and native talent.

The colors are applied with artists' ordinary sable brushes. After the decorations are completed, Rozane Ware is ready for the "test of fire," the last step in the manufacturing process.

Again encased in protecting molds, the pieces are placed in immense kilns, where they are subjected to the fierce heat of 1800 degrees Fahrenheit. After the first "firing" they are plunged into a solution of glaze, which not only gives them their beautiful gloss, but makes the decorations permanent. Then they are given a final "firing," and Rozane Ware, in all its beauty and brilliancy, is ready for the market, to gladden the artistic eye and add to the tasteful ornamentation of the most luxuriously appointed homes.

Vase, 12", Rozane RPCO die stamp #818 (Myers)
$400.00–500.00
Vase, 7", Rozane RPCO die stamp #843, artist initialed
$350.00–450.00
Vase, 5", Rozane RPCO die stamp #874 (W M)
$275.00–375.00

These rare examples of Rozane are highlighted with Aurelian-like orange streaking.

ROW 1:
Vase, 9½" (H S)
$1,800.00–2,000.00
Pillow Vase, 8½"
$1,800.00–2,000.00
Vase, 8½", Rozane Royal seal
(Dunlavy), *$2,000.00–2,250.00*

ROW 2:
Pillow Vase, 9", Rozane RPCO die
stamp #882, *$2,000.00–2,250.00*
Vase, 8", Rozane Royal seal,
(Dunlavy), *$2,000.00–2,250.00*
Pillow Vase, 9", Rozane Royal seal
(Pillsbury), *$1,800.00–2,000.00*

ROW 3:
Vase, 13", Rozane RPCO die (Leffler)
$3,500.00–4,000.00
Vase, 17", Rozane RPCO die stamp
#931 (F. Steele), *$3,000.00–3,500.00*
Vase, 14", Rozane RPCO die stamp,
artist signed, *$2,800.00–3,250.00*

ROSEVILLE ARTISTS AND THEIR SIGNATURES

The signed art pottery in this Volume reveals ciphers that were not listed in Volume I, many of which remain unidentified. Several of these artists initials correspond with some of those from Owens — and it seems likely that they would have migrated to Roseville when art pottery production was discontinued there in 1906. Several well known Roseville artists once worked at Owens: Virginia Adams, A. F. Best, John Butterworth, Charles Chilcote, Frank Ferrel, John Herold, Sarah and Mae Timberlake and many others. It is doubtful that such artists as Fannie Bell, Edith Bell or Cecelia Bloomer would not have continued their work elsewhere during a time when the production of art pottery was at its peak.

G. B. (unknown)

G B

Della Robbia

F.B., F.A.B. (unknown)

F B , F A B

Della Robbia

C.B. (unknown)

C B

Crocus

E.B., E.R.B. (unknown)

E B   E R B

Della Robbia

E.C. (unknown)

E C

Della Robbia

Katy Duvall

K D

Della Robbia

Caroline Steinle

S

Decorated Matt

Goldie

-G- -Goldε-

Della Robbia

William Hall

W. H.

Rozane

Claude Leffler

CL CLL

Azurean, Rozane

C. Mitchell

C Mitchell

Rozane

M.N. (unknown)

MN

Rozane

C. Neff

C NEFF

Rosane
(several Neff signatures
began with the letter C)

E.T. (unknown)

E T

Woodland

ROW 1: Vase, 5½", Rozane RPCO die stamp #872 ....$175.00–200.00

Vase, 6½", Rozane RPCO die stamp #840/6 ....$125.00–150.00

Vase, 9", Rozane Royal seal, (G. Gerwick) $150.00–175.00

Vase, 8", Rozane Royal seal, (C. Neff) $200.00–250.00

Pillow Vase, 5", Rozane RPCO die stamp #904/7 ....$150.00–175.00

ROW 2: Ewer, 7½", Rozane RPCO die stamp #857/x $150.00–175.00

Vase, 10", Rozane Royal seal, (C. Neff) $175.00–200.00

Vase, 13", Rozane RPCO die stamp #837/3 ....$200.00–275.00

Vase, 11", Rozane RPCO die stamp #902/3 (CLL) $250.00–275.00

Ewer, 7½", #950 ....$150.00–175.00

ROW 3: Vase, 10½", #5 ....$200.00–250.00

Paperweight, 4½", Rozane Royal seal (V. Adams) $225.00–275.00

Jardiniere, 9½", no mark $150.00–200.00

Vase, 11", #7 ....$300.00–350.00

The artist's signature on #4, Row 1 & #2, Row 2 was plainly C. Neff not G (Grace) which is more familiar to Roseville collectors.

11

ROZANE, 1900s

ROW 1:
Vase, 7¼", Rozane Ware seal,
(V. Adams), *$175.00–200.00*
Tankard, 10½", Rozane RPCO #821
(CF), *$450.00–500.00*
Candlestick, 9", Rozane Ware seal,
(J. Imlay), *$225.00–275.00*
Vase, 7½", Rozane RPCO die stamp
#836, *$150.00–175.00*

ROW 2:
Vase, 8", Rozane Ware seal,
(Dunlavy), *$2,000.00–2,250.00*
Pillow Vase 9", Rozane RPCO die
stamp #882 (MT)
$2,000.00–2,250.00
Vase, 7½", (G. Gerwick)
$225.00–275.00

ROW 3:
Vase, Rozane RPCO die stamp #891
$2,750.00–3,000.00
Vase, 15", Rozane Ware wafer,
(L. M.), *$750.00–850.00*
Vase, 14", Rozane RPCO die stamp
#891 (W. Myers), *$750.00–850.00*

Vase, rare sepia-tone glazing, Rozane Ware seal #36,
(Pillsbury), *$700.00–750.00*
Three sided vase, portraying Morning, Noon, and Night,
Rozane Royal seal, 1213/188, (EA), *$1,250.00–1,500.00*
Mug, 5", (Dunlavy)
$900.00–1,100.00

ROZANE, 1900s

ROW 1:
Letter Holder, 3½", Rozane Royal seal, (C. Neff), *$250.00–300.00*
Mug, 4½", "Rubba Dub Dub, Three Men in a Tub," stenciled decoration, Rozane RPCO die stamp #856, *$200.00–250.00*
Bud Vase, 6½", Rozane RPCO die stamp #875, (WH), *$250.00–300.00*
Bud Vase, 6½", Rozane RPCO #915, artist signed, *$125.00–150.00*
Mug, 5", Rozane Royal seal, (G. Gerwick), *$225.00–250.00*
Mug, 4½", Rozane RPCO die stamp #856 (D), *$150.00–175.00*

ROW 2:
Vase, 10", (M. Timberlake) *$750.00–850.00*
Vase, 11", Rozane Royal seal, (W. Myers), *$450.00–500.00*
Ewer, 10½", Rozane Royal seal, (C. Neff), *$350.00–400.00*

ROW 3:
Vase 13", Rozane Ware seal, (Imlay), *$400.00–450.00*
Tankard, 14", Rozane Ware seal, (Imlay), *$500.00–550.00*
Vase, 18½", Rozane RPCO #865, (W. Myers), *$500.00–600.00*
Vase, 15", Rozane Royal seal, (V. Adams)*, *$500.00–600.00*
Vase, 10½", Rozane Royal seal (G. Gerwick)*, *$500.00–600.00*
*Note rare color effect

Who wouldn't have taken advantage of this special offer from the Roseville Company?

A VERY SPECIAL OFFER
(Reprinted form a circa 1900 Roseville ad)

"That the delight and value of Rozane, as a true art pottery, may become universally known, we wish to place one piece in your hands, and our booklet in the hands of your friends. We ask you to help us do this. If, therefore, you will have the kindness to send us the full names and correct addresses of ten persons who admire art pottery, or who might become purchasers of Rozane, we will, immediately upon receipt of your list, accompanied by one dollar to cover the cost of packing and shipping, forward you the handsome Envelope Receiver here illustrated. This Receiver is absolutely worth $3.00. It is genuine Rozane Royal, having the same lustrous finish. One of the very prettiest uses to which this holder can be put is to make it a Receiver for letters brought by the postman. It is very handsome upon a desk or hall table, and letters taken from this dainty holder seem all the more welcome, while the appearance of the desk or table is greatly improved by the orderly habit of dropping the mail into this luxurious Receiver."

ROSEVILLE POTTERY

3" x 8¼", black lacquered wood faced with a brass plate attached with square brass brads. The metal plate has a black background with a border of two gold lines. "Roseville Pottery" is in red outlined with gold. Made by the American Art Works, Inc., Coshocton, Ohio, who also made Coca-Cola items in the early 1900s. *$1,200.00–1,500.00*

ROW 1:
Bud Vase, 7½", Rozane RPCO die stamp #841/3, (MN), *$150.00–175.00*
Bud Vase, 8", Rozane Royal seal, (C. Neff), *$150.00–175.00*
Pillow Vase, 7", Rozane Royal seal, (J. Imlay), *$300.00–350.00*
Vase, 8½", Rozane Ware seal, (Timberlake), *$150.00–175.00*
Vase, 6½", Rozane Ware seal, (B. Myers), *$150.00–175.00*

ROW 2:
Vase, 8½", Rozane Ware seal *$200.00–250.00*
Vase, 10½", Rozane Royal seal, (W. Myers), *$275.00–325.00*
Pillow Vase, 8½", Rozane Ware seal, (V. Adams), *$300.00–350.00*
Vase, 11", Rozane Ware seal, (B. Myers), *$225.00–275.00*
Vase, 10½", no mark *$225.00–275.00*

ROW 3:
Vase 14", Rozane Royal seal, (H. Pillsbury), *$500.00–600.00*
Ewer, 16", Rozane RPCO die stamp #858 (W. Myers), *$800.00–900.00*
Tankard, 15½", Rozane Royal seal, (V. Adams), *$800.00–900.00*
Mug, 6", Rozane Royal seal, artist signed, *$250.00–300.00*

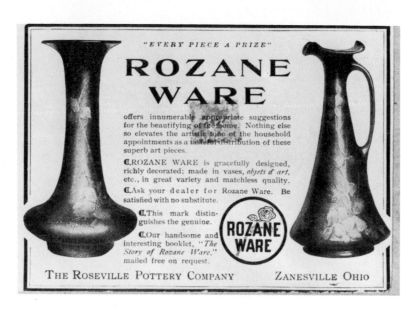

ROW 1:
Vase, 8", Rozane Ware seal, (H.P.)
$200.00–250.00
Vase, 9½", no mark, (C. Neff)
$200.00–250.00
Vase, 11½", Rozane RPCO die
stamp #833/3, *$250.00–300.00*
Chocolate Pot, 9½", Rozane RPCO
die stamp #936/7, artist signed
$400.00–500.00

ROW 2:
Mug, 4", Rozane RPCO die stamp,
#856/6, *$125.00–150.00*
Mug, 6", Rozane Ware seal
$200.00–250.00
Pillow Vase, 7", no mark
$300.00–350.00
Mug, 4", Rozane RPCO die stamp
#856/2, *$125.00–150.00*

ROW 3:
Tankard, 16", Rozane Ware seal, (J.
Imlay), *$550.00–650.00*
Vase, 16", no mark
$500.00–600.00
Tankard, 15½", Rozane Royal seal,
(W. Myers), *$450.00–500.00*

LIGHT ROZANE

ROW 1:
Bowl, 3", (M T)
$200.00–250.00
Vase, 4", (W M)
$175.00–225.00
Bowl, 5"
$175.00–200.00
Mug, 5", Rozane Royal seal,
(Pillsbury), *$400.00–450.00*

ROW 2:
Pillow Vase, 6½", Rozane Royal seal
$375.00–425.00
Vase, 8½", Rozane Ware seal
$1,750.00–2,000.00
Pillow Vase, 7", Rozane Royal seal,
(M. Timberlake), *$300.00–375.00*

ROW 3:
Vase, 6½", Rozane Royal seal,
(V. Adams), *$275.00–325.00*
Vase, 13", Rozane Royal seal, (W.
Myers), *$350.00–450.00*
Vase, 18", (M T)
$900.00–1,100.00
Vase, 14", Rozane Ware seal, (M. F.)
$850.00–950.00
Vase, 8½", Rozane Royal seal,
(H. Pillsbury), *$325.00–375.00*

Jardiniere, 5"
$175.00–200.00
Vase, 11½", (W. Myers)
$400.00–450.00
Vase, 15", (M. Timberlake)
$1,500.00–1,750.00

LIGHT ROZANE

ROW 1: Sugar Bowl, 4½"...$175.00–200.00

      Teapot, 8", #60, (RHEAD) $1,500.00–1,750.00

      Mug, 5", (M. Timberlake) $300.00–350.00

ROW 2: Vase, 8", Rozane Royal seal, (J. Imlay) $300.00–350.00

      Vase, 8", Rozane Royal seal, (J. Imlay) $350.00–400.00

      Vase, 10", Rozane Royal seal, (W. Myers) $450.00–500.00

      Vase, 10", Rozane Royal seal, (W. Myers) $300.00–350.00

      Vase, 8½", Rozane Royal seal, (W. Myers) $275.00–325.00

ROW 3: Tankard, 11", Rozane Royal seal, (C. Mitchell)...$550.00–650.00

      Vase, 11", Rozane Royal seal (H. Pillsbury) $450.00–550.00

      Tankard, 16", Rozane Royal seal, (L. Mitchell) $1,000.00–1,250.00

      Vase, 10½", Rozane Royal seal, (J. Imlay)...$350.00–400.00

      Tankard, 10", Rozane Royal seal, (J. Imlay)...$850.00–950.00

Paper collectibles such as these display invitations, booklets, and stationery items are always of interest to collectors.
$20.00–35.00

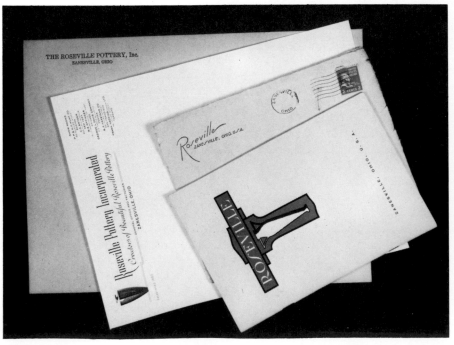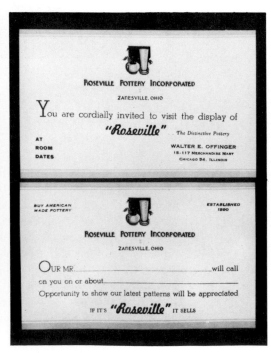

VASE ASSORTMENT #24

Vase, 8", #107 ....$300.00–325.00
Vase, 9", #102 ....$325.00–375.00
Vase, 9", #110 ....$325.00–375.00
Vase, 8", #108 ....$325.00–375.00
Vase, 7", #109 ....$275.00–325.00

AZUREAN, 1902

ROW 1:
Vase, 9", no mark
$2,000.00–2,250.00

ROW 2:
Candlestick, 9", no mark (V. Adams)
$475.00–575.00
Vase, 7½", RPCO die stamp #4, (Leffler)
$475.00–575.00
Mug, RPCO die stamp #4
$425.00–475.00

ROW 3:
Vase, 14", Rozane Ware seal, (W. Myers)
$1,100.00–1,250.00
Vase, 18", RPCO #865, (B. Myers)
$1,000.00–1,250.00
Vase, 15½", #822/7, (Leffler)
$1,000.00–1,150.00

OLYMPIC, 1905

Top Right:

ROW 1:
Pitcher, 7", Rozane Olympic Pottery black ink mark, "Ulysses at the Table of Circle" $2,000.00–2,250.00
Pitcher, 7", "Pandora Brought to Earth"..$1,850.00–2,150.00

ROW 2:
Vase, 14½", "Persia and Ionia Yoked to the Chariot of Xesxes"..$3,500.00–4,000.00
Vase, 20", "Juno Commanding the Sun to Set" $4,000.00–4,500.00

MARA, 1904
ROZANE MARA...where the Rainbow Comes From

"As changing as the sea, from which it derives its name, and from which, like an opalesque and dainty shell, it seems to have caught every morning hue of iridescence when the sunbeam kissed the spray, Rozane Mara is one of the most decorative as well as one of the most pleasing results yet obtained at the Roseville Potteries."

"Studying to obtain the exquisite rainbow tints seen in rarest pieces of old Italian glass, our artist chemist evolved this oddity. The surface, in texture much resembling the lining of the ocean's rarest shells, is somewhat irregular, presenting surfaces most favorable for catching every ray of light, throwing it back in all lustrous shades imaginable. With all this play of colors, Rozane Mara is subdued and in good taste, the prevailing tones running under and through the iridescence being odd reds, varying from pale rose tints to the deepest magentas, the soft tones of gray and opal suggesting the pearly surface of a shell, being always present."

— From an early Rozane Ware catalogue —

Bottom Left:

Vase, 13", no mark $1,500.00–1,800.00
Bowl, 4", no mark $1,100.00–1,300.00
Vase, 13", no mark $1,500.00–2,000.00

Bottom Right:

Vase, 5½", no mark $1,400.00–1,750.00
Vase, 5½", #13 ....$1,300.00–1,650.00

21

MONGOL, 1904

"Rozane Mongol is the name found upon all pieces of Rozane decorated in the rich, beautiful red, known as 'Sang de Boeuf' and which, until very lately, was produced only by the ancient Chinese. For centuries, potters have endeavored to reproduce it, and only in the present generation has this been done. In honor of the famous Mongolian potters who first produced, in pottery, this color of wonderful richness and permanence, the name Mongol was given to this variety of Rozane.

It is a peculiar fact that any one shape reproduced in a number of styles is more admired in this beautiful Mongol red than in any better known color of the day. While ornamentation and design are attractive, especially when viewed by themselves, as single elements of a perfect whole, nothing is better, in the furnishing of a harmonious room, than art objects in a simple color, wisely placed to lend just the right, pleasing effect to the eye.

A late writer, comparing vases of plain color and those decorated, gives a vivid figure by comparing those of one color to the single musical notes which, combined, produce a harmony. Were each a complete tune, simultaneously sounded, the result would be a jangling discord.

Thus, while elaborate decoration is desirable for certain places (against a plain wall, a drapery of plain material or in a niche by itself), as a unit in the decoration of an entire room, the vase of single color, or in varying hues of the same color, is often most pleasing — most harmonious.

To this harmony is added still another result upon a room by the addition of a piece of Rozane Mongol — its effect of richness.

It is the famous, long-sought red of the Chinese revealing many harmonious hues made brilliant by any reflections, in its glaze, from window or artificial light, and wherever placed the Mongol vase imparts a rich, luxurious touch of warmth, needed in every room where a feeling of comfort is desired."

— From an early Rozane Ware catalogue —

Top Right:

ROW 1:
3-Handled Mug, 6", Rozane Mongol seal $700.00–850.00
Vase, 5", Rozane Mongol seal..$500.00–600.00

ROW 2:
Vase, 10½", small paper label #C-16..$1,100.00–1,250.00
Vase, 14", Rozane Mongol seal...$900.00–1,100.00
Vase, 16", Rozane Mongol seal...$900.00–1,150.00

Bottom Left:

Vase, 8", Rozane Ware seal..$800.00–900.00
Vase, 10½", no mark $850.00–950.00

Bottom Right:

Experimental Vase, 7", Rozane Mongol seal #120 ....$2,200.00–2,500.00
Vase, 2½", no mark $400.00–500.00

WOODLAND, 1905

ROW 1:
Vase, 6", Rozane Ware seal
$550.00–650.00
Vase, 6½", no mark
$575.00–650.00
Vase, 6½", Rozane Ware seal
$575.00–650.00
Vase, 7", Rozane Ware Woodland
seal, $550.00–600.00

ROW 2:
Vase, 9", Rozane Ware Woodland
seal, $650.00–750.00
Vase, 9", Rozane Ware Woodland
seal, $650.00–750.00
Vase, 11", Rozane Ware Woodland
seal, $700.00–900.00
Vase, 11½", Rozane Ware seal
$750.00–950.00
Vase, 10", Rozane Ware seal
$700.00–800.00
Vase, 9", no mark
$600.00–700.00

ROW 3:
Vase, 13", Rozane Ware Woodland
seal, $1,200.00–1,500.00
Vase, 19", Rozane Ware Woodland
seal, $1,800.00–2,200.00
Vase, 15½", Rozane Ware Woodland,
(E T), $1,000.00–1,200.00
Vase, 15", Rozane Ware Woodland,
$1,100.00–1,300.00

ROZANE WOODLAND...Ancient Spirit of Modern Art. We do not deny that the resemblance of Rozane Woodland to one of the oldest and rarest of Chinese potteries is no accident. While Woodland is not an attempt at imitation of the old Chinese Celadon, familiarity with the latter, and with its exquisite qualities, was inspiration to the artist who created the idea of Rozane Woodland. Old Celadon, like Woodland, was decorated by incising either floral or conventional designs in the moist clay, or biscuit, after moulding, and was further ornamented by studs or dots. The old Celadon was very hard, opaque, closely akin to stoneware, and covered with a partially translucent enamel. There were vases of gray earth shading into browns and yellows and scattered with little laminae of mica, or sometimes picked with tiny points, almost imperceptible. The value of old pieces in this style is almost inestimable.

The description of Rozane Woodland is almost identical with this of the old Chinese ware, except that Woodland has not the mica. The laminae mentioned, however, are daintily picked into the surface of the softly shaded mat background, lending just an agreeable relief from its plainness, which is further broken by the dots or "studs," while the enameled designs stand out in pleasant contrast. The latter are usually in foliage hues, the browns resembling late autumn woodlands, when the dun, frost-exposed oak leaves — brown, mellow and glossy — still cling, rustling, in final glory, to the trees.

Rozane Woodland is exceptionally beautiful in every point that contributes to the excellence of an art pottery. It is a pleasure to present this as our final argument for the true worth of Rozane.

— From an early Rozane Ware catalogue —

Vase, 6", no mark
This vase contained this note of verification: Bought from daughter of J. F. Weaver, Vice-president of first Rv officers. This vase made by Roseville Pottery and designed by Fudjiyama. (signed) Evan Purviance
$1,000.00–1,250.00
Pitcher, 7½", no mark
$1,100.00–1,300.00
WOODLAND Vase, 11", Rozane Ware seal
$1,800.00–2,000.00

FUDJI, 1906

ROW 1:
Vase, 9", no mark
$1,250.00–1,500.00
Vase, 10½", Rozane Ware seal
$1,300.00–1,500.00
Vase, 10", Rozane Ware seal, (E)
$1,300.00–1,450.00

ROW 2:
Vase, 15", Fudjiyama ink stamp
$1,000.00–1,250.00
Jardiniere, 9", Fudjiyama ink stamp
$1,100.00–1,350.00
Vase, 11", Fudjiyama ink stamp
$850.00–950.00
Vase, 9", Fudjiyama ink stamp
$750.00–850.00

DELLA ROBBIA, 1906

ROW 1:
Teapot, 6", Rozane Ware seal, (E B)
$1,100.00–1,300.00
Teapot, 5½", Rozane Ware seal
Inscription: If a woman says she will, she will, depend on it. But if she says she won't, she won't and there's an end on't, (K D and E R)
$1,100.00–1,500.00
Teapot, 6", Rozane Ware seal
$1,100.00–1,250.00

ROW 2:
Mug, 4½", Rozane Ware seal, and Della Robbia paper label, (H S)
$500.00–750.00
Pitcher, 8", (K E)
$3,500.00–4,500.00
Mug, 4½", (F B)
$500.00–750.00

Paper label found on first Mug in
Row 2 above.

ROW 1:
Tankard, 10½", (H S)
$1,700.00–2,100.00
Teapot, 6½", Rozane Ware seal
$1,200.00–1,300.00
Tankard, 10½", Rozane Ware seal
Inscription: A Chirping Cup is my Matin Song. And the Vesper Bell is My Bowl. Ding Dong! (M F)
$1,350.00–1,550.00

ROW 2:
Vase, 10", (M H)
$3,500.00–4,500.00
Vase, 11", Rozane Ware seal, (G C)?
$2,500.00–2,750.00
Vase, 9", Rozane Ware seal, (H. Smith)
$1,500.00–2,000.00

DELLA ROBBIA, 1906

ROW 1:
Vase, 8", Rozane Ware seal, (G B)
$3,250.00–4,000.00
Teapot, 8", Rozane Ware seal, (K)
$1,200.00–1,500.00
Vase, 8½", Rozane Ware seal, (M E)
$3,000.00–4,000.00

ROW 2:
Mug, 4", (K D)
$500.00–700.00
Jar, 8", (shown without lid), (-G-)
$2,250.00–2,500.00
Vase, 9½", (E C)
$1,250.00–1,750.00
Bowl, 8" x 2½", (H S)
$1,300.00–1,500.00
Letter Holder, 3½", no mark
$650.00–750.00

ROW 3:
Vase, 15", Rozane Ware seal, (–Golde–)
$5,000.00–6,000.00
Vase, 14", Rozane Ware seal,
(H. Smith), *$6,000.00–8,000.00*
Vase, 11½", (F B)
$6,000.00–8,000.00
Vase, 11½", (H L)
$3,000.00–4,000.00

Vase, 19", no mark, (H L)
$6,000.00–8,000.00

Vase, 12", Rozane Ware seal, (E C)
$8,000.00–12,000.00

Vase, 8½", Rozane Ware seal,
(H. Smith), *$4,000.00–5,000.00*

Vase, 14", Rozane Ware seal,
$1,200.00–1,400.00
Pot, 3", no mark
$900.00–1,100.00

This pot was identified from a series of line drawings of unusual Crystalis shapes found among the Roseville files. Several of these have been reproduced here.

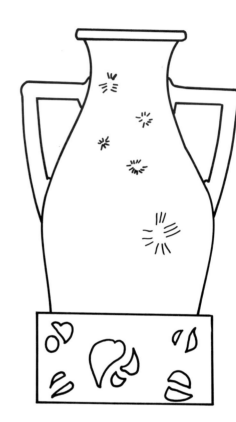

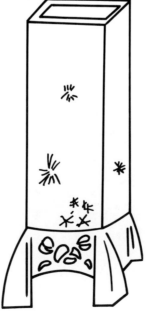

CRYSTALIS, 1906

Candlestick, 9", Rozane Ware Mongol seal (!)
$800.00–900.00
Vase, 12½", Rozane Ware paper label (below)
$1,300.00–1,500.00
Vase, 13", no mark, *$1,250.00–1,500.00*
Vase, 11", no mark, *$1,300.00–1,450.00*
Vase, 5½", Rozane Ware Mongol seal, (mismarked pieces are occasionally found)
$800.00–900.00

ROW 1:
Vase, 3½", (H. Rhead)
$350.00–450.00
WATER LILY Planter/Liner, 4", squeezebag
decoration, *$300.00–400.00*
GOLD Vase, 7", #501
$250.00 350.00
MARA Vase, 5½"
$600.00–800.00

ROW 2:
Vase, 11", sgraffito decoration
$900.00–1,100.00
DECORATED LANDSCAPE Vase, 9",
sgraffito and squeezebag, artist signed
$1,000.00–1,300.00
Vase, 8½", stencil technique
$500.00–800.00
Vase, determined recently to be
Weller Pottery.
Vase, 12", transfer with gold, sometimes
referred to as Jeanette
$400.00–500.00

BLUE TEAPOTS

ROW 3:
Mug, 6", no mark
$200.00–250.00
Pot, 8", no mark
$300.00–350.00
Pot, 7", no mark
$350.00–400.00
Pot, 4", no mark
$200.00–250.00

Specials as indicated in the Roseville catalogue are those decorated with a stencil over a highly refined body closely resembling fine painted china. Early Rozane shapes were often used, which determines this ware to be from the early 1900s. Grapes are the more common motif, but in the portrait vase on the following page, the artist has utilized the same technique.

Decorated Art is a rather broad term adopted by collectors to refer to the less detailed, often Art Nouveau style of decoration as shown in the photo at the top of the opposite page. Often gold tracing is used for a lovely accent. The molds for these are also early 1900.

SPECIAL, early 1900s

Mug, 5", no mark
$200.00–250.00
Tankard, 12", no mark,
(P. Gasper), *$400.00–450.00*
Mug, 5", no mark
$175.00–225.00
Tankard, 15½", RPCO #884
$550.00–600.00

DECORATED ART, 1900s

ROW 1:
Jardiniere, 8", no mark
$300.00–350.00
Vase, 12½", #20
$400.00–450.00
Jardiniere, 6", no mark
$175.00–225.00

ROW 2:
Jardiniere, 10", #448
$300.00–350.00
This unusual mark also appeared on this item.

Vase, 16", no mark
$1,250.00–1,500.00

Pillow Vase, 9", Rozane RPCO #882
$3,000.00–3,500.00
Vase, 9", no mark
$350.00–450.00

EGYPTO, 1905
CHLORON, 1907
MATT GREEN before 1916

TOP:
Hanging Basket, 9", MATT GREEN,
no mark, *$150.00–200.00*

ROW 1:
Planter/Liner, 4", MATT GREEN, #510
$125.00–150.00
Candlestick, 4", Rozane EGYPTO,
Roseville P co, Zanesville, Ohio
$150.00–175.00
3-way Creamer, 3½", Rozane EGYPTO
seal, *$175.00–200.00*
Bud vase, 5½", Rozane EGYPTO seal
$250.00–300.00
Bowl, 3", no mark
$150.00–175.00

ROW 2:
Jardiniere, 5½", #487
$200.00–250.00
Vase, 7", CHLORON ink stamp and
TRPCo (see Decorated Art),
$500.00–600.00
Vase, 9", Indented mark, CHLORON
$450.00–550.00

ROW 3:
Vase, 12½", Rozane EGYPTO seal
$475.00–525.00
Pitcher, 12", Rozane EGYPTO seal
$400.00–450.00
Circle Jug, 11", Rozane EGYPTO seal
$600.00–700.00
Planter, 5½", MATT GREEN, no mark
$200.00–250.00

Egypto or Chloron? These are two very difficult lines to distinguish. These green glazes vary from those with a "rubbery" effect to others with "pepper" dots — from very dark to unusually light. Quite probably Chloron evolved from the early Egypto and perhaps in later years became simply Matt Green. The only advice we can offer on unmarked items is to check catalogue reprints. Rozane shapes won't always indicate Rozane Egypto — for instance Row 2 #2 is marked Chloron. In Row 2, the jardiniere with the cameo may be Chloron, but we rather feel that it is Cameo. Referring to page 152, Volume I, the cameo with peacock motif has been found on a pedestal with a jardiniere like this one.

CHLORON, 1907

ROW 1:
Vase, 6½", no mark
$200.00–250.00
Vase, 12", no mark
$350.00–450.00
Vase, 9", CHLORON ink stamp
$450.00–500.00

MATT GREEN, before 1916

ROW 2:
Pot/Liner, 3", no mark
$40.00–50.00
Pot/Liner, 3", no mark
$45.00–50.00
Pot/Liner, 4", no mark
$40.00–50.00
Gate, 5" x 8", no mark
$35.00–50.00
Pot/Frog, 2½", no mark
$40.00–50.00

ROW 3:
Jardiniere, 6", no mark
$100.00–125.00
Tobacco Jar, 6", no mark
$150.00–200.00
Planter/Liner, 4" x 8", no mark
$150.00–250.00
Jardiniere, 5½", #456, Roseville
Pottery Co., Zanesville, Ohio, size 5
on paper label, *$150.00–250.00*

EGYPTO, 1905

ROW 4:
Pitcher Vase, 11", Rozane Ware seal
$300.00–350.00
Lamp base, 10", no mark
$1,000.00–1,250.00
Vase, 6½", Rozane EGYPTO seal
$200.00–250.00
Pitcher, 7", Rozane EGYPTO seal
$250.00–300.00
Vase, 5½", Rozane EGYPTO seal
$250.00–300.00

ROZANE EGYPTO...Thought Made Permanent in Pottery. Rozane Egypto may be classed as one of the oddest styles of Rozane, although its soft finish and coloring, in varying shades of old greens, suggest a very beautiful color found in some of the rarest and most ancient potteries of old Egypt. The shapes and decorations, too, are reproductions of Egyptian art antiques. Each piece of Rozane Egypto expresses a complete thought of its artist, savoring of the restfulness and freedom of nature. Through the shades of old green are seen glintings of those rich violets and blues which often entered into the colorings of rarest old Egyptian pieces. The prevailing color of these latter was a green which came to be almost as famous as the old red of the Chinese.

— Rozane Egypto is indispensable in a collection of Rozanes — or of any pottery. Not only is the color itself peculiarly attractive and restful, but the forms in this variety, like all Rozanes, are graceful and well proportioned. The low modelings of matt decoration retaining the prevailing hues, contribute effectively to its beauty. — *From an early Rozane Ware catalogue* —

PAULEO, 1914

From a booklet entitled "Pauleo Pottery" presented by the Roseville Company in 1916 comes the information that up until that time, at least, Pauleo was never decorated. The company emphasized this point elaborately, stating that its aesthetic value was accented by its simplicity — a "leaving off of adornment." But its unusual, varied glazes stirred enough excitement to make it a very popular seller. A Pauleo Pottery shop was opened in New York on 50th and 5th Ave. George Young, Harry Rhead and C. E. Offinger themselves took charge of its production. It was only during the next few years that decoration was added the Pauleo line.

"Creations that are Superb as Gifts — Roseville Pottery"
Company booklet

as Gifts — Roseville Pottery

And there is such a variety of exquisite pieces from which to choose! An entrancing wealth of designs, making the heart rejoice! Such a wonderful ensemble of shapes and sizes and tints of delicate grey and green and blue, that one need never be at a loss in selecting the gift supreme—ROSEVILLE pottery!

The charm of contour and color that ROSEVILLE pottery reveals so abundantly places it at once among the most cherished possessions. The sentiment it conveys cannot be measured by its cost. The recipient of a gift of ROSEVILLE will always treasure it and the giver may be assured that it is in perfect taste for any occasion.

Treasures With a Charm of Their Own

[13]

PAULEO, 1914

ROW 1:
Vase, 9", no mark $500.00–600.00
Vase, 12", Ginger Jar paper label (shown at right) $500.00–650.00
Vase, 9", no mark $500.00–600.00

ROW 2:
Vase, 18½", Pauleo seal $1,000.00–1,250.00
Vase, 19", no mark..$1,100.00–1,250.00
Vase 20½", no mark..$1,200.00–1,400.00

PAULEO, 1914

ROW 1:
Vase, 17", Grey lustre shading, red berries, green leaves, no mark *$1,000.00–1,200.00*
Vase, 14", Pearl grey lustre, orange flowers, green stems and leaves, no mark, *$900.00–1,000.00*

ROW 2:
Vase, 17½", Gold mottling, no mark *$1,000.00–1,200.00*
Vase, 19", Lavender lustre, purple grapes, green leaves and vines, no mark, *$1,150.00–1,250.00*
Vase, 16½", Grey to lavender glazing, no mark, *$950.00–1,150.00*

Left:
Old company photo showing Pauleo shapes.

PAULEO, 1914

ROW 1:
Vase, 16½", Pauleo seal (mark #11, Vol. 1), *$950.00–1,150.00*
Vase, 14", no mark
$900.00–1,100.00
Vase, 16½", no mark
$950.00–1,150.00

ROW 2:
Vase, 15½", no mark
$1,100.00–1,300.00
Vase, 17", no mark
$1,100.00–1,350.00

Bottom Left:
Vase, 12", undetermined line, Victorian Art Pottery shape, no mark
$1,200.00–1,500.00
Vase, 12", decal decoration, undetermined line,
$600.00–750.00

Bottom Right:
Vase, 19", #340
$1,200.00–1,300.00
Bowl, 3", no mark
$400.00–500.00
Vase, 19", no mark
$1,150.00–1,250.00

CARNELIAN, early 1900s
COLONIAL, early 1900s
HOLLAND, before 1916

ROW 1:
CARNELIAN Shaving Mug, 4",
no mark, *$65.00–75.00*
CARNELIAN Mush Bowl, 3" &
Pitcher, 5½", *$80.00–100.00*
CARNELIAN Toothbrush Holder,
5", no mark, *$60.00–70.00*
CARNELIAN Soap Dish, 4",
no mark, *$75.00–85.00*

ROW 2:
COLONIAL Soap Dish, 4", no mark
$80.00–90.00
VENETIAN Salesman's Sample,
marked Venetian, #3 (?)
$70.00–80.00
CARNELIAN Shaving Mug, 4"
$65.00–75.00
HOLLAND Pitcher, 12", no mark
$250.00–350.00

ROW 3:
CARNELIAN Pitcher, 12" & Bowl,
15½", no mark, *$350.00–450.00*
COLONIAL, combinet, 12",
no mark, *$300.00–350.00*

Below: This Holland stein set was a promotional item offered by a beer company.

CARNELIAN, early 1900s

ROW 1:
Pitcher, 4", no mark
$50.00–60.00
Pitcher, 5", no mark
$75.00–85.00
"Wild Rose" Pitcher, 9", no mark
$125.00–150.00
Pitcher with Wheat, 5½", no mark
$75.00–85.00
Pitcher with Corn, 5", no mark
$100.00–125.00

ROW 2:
"Corn" Pitcher, 6", no mark
$125.00–150.00
"Our Leader" Jardiniere, base dia.
4½", no mark, *$95.00–110.00*
"Our Leader" Jardiniere, base dia.
4", #119, *$100.00–125.00*

COLONIAL, early 1900s

ROW 3:
Pitcher, 7½", no mark
$100.00–125.00
Pitcher, 11", no mark
$175.00–250.00
Bowl, 16", no mark
$150.00–200.00
Toothbrush, 5", no mark
$85.00–95.00

HOLLAND, before 1916

Powder Jar, 3", no mark
$100.00–125.00
Tankard, #2, 9½", no mark
$125.00–175.00
Pitcher, #1, 6½", no mark
$175.00–200.00
Mug, 4", no mark
$65.00–75.00

Shiny Aztec or Crocus...whatever the term you choose to refer to the ware in Rows 2 and 3, opposite (we find nothing official), consider it synonymous with "rare," "beautiful," and certainly "desirable" for your collection. Although a few shapes from this line are also used in the Aztec line (page 60, *Early Roseville*) the same shapes were also used in Della Robbia (page 59, *Early Roseville*) as well as some Rozane lines. Some shapes, Row 2 #1 and Row 3 #2, seem exclusive to this line; the decoration is slip work, rather than squeezebag.

Around 1913–14 pottery journals reported that the industry overall was booming. New techniques and innovations were being utilized, and the emphasis put on decoration rather than shape. More than likely Crocus emerged around this time, although it may have been a few years earlier.

AZTEC, 1915

ROW 1:

Vase, 11½", no mark *$350.00–450.00*
Vase, 10½", no mark *$300.00–400.00*
Vase 9½", no mark *$225.00–275.00*

ROW 4:

Vase, 9", (E) *$425.00–475.00*
Vase, 11" (R) *$400.00–500.00*
Vase, 11", no mark *$400.00–500.00*
Vase, 9", no mark *$375.00–425.00*
Vase, 8", (R) *$400.00–500.00*

CROCUS

ROW 2:

Vase, 7", no mark *$300.00–350.00*
Vase, 9½", no mark (C B) *$425.00–475.00*
Vase, 9", no mark *$375.00–425.00*
Vase, 7", no mark *$300.00–350.00*

ROW 3:

Vase, 9", (G S) *$350.00–400.00*
Vase, 7", no mark *$350.00–400.00*
Vase, 6", Rozane Ware seal, (P D) *$300.00–350.00*
Letter Receiver, undetermined line, 3½", no mark *$200.00–250.00*

41

EARLY PITCHERS, before 1916

ROW 1:
Utility Pitcher, 6½", no mark $75.00–85.00
Pitcher, 8", no mark..$95.00–110.00

ROW 2:
"The Grape" Pitcher, 6", "Compliments of Magee Furnace Co.,"
    (This particular pitcher was a promotional item.) $150.00–175.00
"The Boy" Pitcher, 7½", no mark $275.00–375.00
"The Grape" Pitcher, 6", no mark..$125.00–150.00

ROW 3:
"Goldenrod" Pitcher, 9½", no mark $125.00–150.00
"The Mill" Pitcher, 8", no mark...$275.00–325.00
"Wild Rose" Pitcher, 9½", no mark $125.00–150.00

EARLY PITCHERS, before 1916

ROW 1:
"The Bridge" Pitcher, 6", no mark
$125.00–150.00
"Iris" Pitcher, 7", no mark
$200.00–250.00
Blended "Bridge" Pitcher, 6", no mark
$125.00–150.00

ROW 2:
"Landscape" Pitcher, 7½", no mark
$125.00–150.00
Undecorated "Tulip" Pitcher, R #18,
U.S.A., 1930s reissue, *$100.00–125.00*
"Tulip" Pitcher, 7½", no mark
$125.00–150.00

ROW 3:
"The Cow" Pitcher, 7½", no mark
$300.00–350.00
"The Cow" Pitcher, 6½", no mark, (rare)
$300.00–400.00
"The Cow" Pitcher, 7½", no mark
$300.00–350.00

"Poppy" Pitcher, 9", #11.............................*$150.00–175.00*
"Poppy" Pitcher, 9", #141...........................*$150.00–175.00*

BLENDED GLAZED & EARLY PITCHERS

ROW 1:
Vase, 7", no mark
$75.00–100.00
Tankard, 12", #890
$150.00–200.00
Vase, 6½", no mark
$75.00–100.00

ROW 2:
GERMAN COOKING WARE Pitcher,
3", no mark, *$60.00–70.00*
Vase, 3", no mark
$75.00–85.00
Vase, 5½", no mark
$85.00–95.00
Vase, 4", #817
$95.00–110.00

ROW 3:
"The Owl" Pitcher, 6½", no mark
$300.00–400.00
Blended Pitcher, 7", no mark
$100.00–125.00
Blended "Grape" Pitcher, 6", no mark
$100.00–125.00

ROW 4;
Blended "Landscape" Pitcher, 7½",
no mark, *$125.00–150.00*
"Wild Rose" with gold tracing, 9",
no mark, *$100.00–125.00*
Blended "Holland," 9½", no mark
$150.00–200.00
ROZANE Pitcher, 8½", #886,
(W. Myers), *$300.00–400.00*

CANVASERS OUTFIT, before 1898

This old ad identified these banks as Roseville Pottery, and their Roseville, Ohio, address dates their production before 1898 when the main office was moved to Zanesville.

CANVASERS OUTFIT — Entire outfit, $1.00 ppd. Included: #90 min. umbrella stand, 3" x 7"...50¢ (#91 was shown, the same as #90, different motif); #228 min. cuspidor, 3" wide...20¢ (#219, #221, and #201 was the same cuspidor, different decoration); #315 min. cooking crock...10¢ (ad says "too well known to need comment"); #221 apple bank and #120 orange bank...10¢ each, finished to represent fruit. ANY CANVASER WITH THIS OUTFIT CAN MAKE $4 to $6 PER DAY.

Apple Bank, 2¾" x 3½"......................................*$125.00–150.00*
Apple Bank, 3" x 4" *$125.00–150.00*
Orange Bank, 3¼" x 3½".................................*$125.00–150.00*

BANKS, early 1900s

ROW 1:
Pig, 2½" x 5", no mark
$125.00–150.00
Large Pig, 4" x 5½", no mark
$150.00–200.00
Pig, 3" x 4", "St. Louis, 1904,"
commemorative, *$125.00–175.00*

ROW 2:
Buffalo, 3" x 6", no mark
$150.00–200.00
Dog, 4", no mark
$150.00–200.00
Uncle Sam, 4", no mark
$125.00–150.00
Buffalo, 3" x 6½", no mark
$150.00–200.00

ROW 1:
Jug, 4", "Ye Olden Time," no mark
$75.00–100.00
Monkey Bottle, 5½", no mark
$100.00–125.00
Monkey, 6", no mark
$125.00–150.00
Monkey, 5½", no mark
$100.00–125.00

ROW 2:
Eagle, 2½", no mark
$150.00–175.00
Lion, 2½", no mark
$100.00–125.00
Cat, 4", no mark
$150.00–175.00
Beehive, 3", no mark
$175.00–200.00
Beehive, 2½", no mark
$150.00–175.00

Banks and novelties were produced early in the 1900s in many colors...green, blue, blended, spongeware, and dark brown. Some were hand decorated. By observation, one collector has been able to determine the identity of some of these early unmarked, uncatalogued novelties — the monkey figural bottles and "Ye Old Time" jugs. All are known to exist in the five glaze colors, as well as hand decorated; all had identical bases and were made of the very light clay.

CREMO, 1916

Opposite Page, Left:

Vase, 7", no mark $1,250.00–1,500.00

SYLVAN, 1916

Opposite Page, Right:

Vase, 9½", no mark $325.00–375.00
Jardiniere, 9", no mark $300.00–350.00

TOURIST, before 1916

Opposite Page, Center:

Window Box, 8½" x 19, no mark $3,000.00–3,500.00
Vase, 8", no mark $1,250.00–1,500.00

AUTUMN, before 1916

Opposite Page, Bottom:

ROW 1:
Pitcher, 8½", no mark $320.00–400.00
Toothbrush Holder, 5", no mark $225.00–275.00
Shaving Mug, 4", no mark $225.00–275.00
Soap Dish/Liner, 5½" across, no mark $250.00–300.00

ROW 2:
Wash Bowl, 14½", no mark $300.00–375.00
Pitcher, 12½", no mark $450.00–500.00
   Set $750.00–850.00
Jardiniere, 9½", no mark $500.00–600.00

TOURIST
Unusual Vase, 9" $500.00–600.00
Creamware with olive green shading, black scene.

NOVELTY STEINS, before 1916

Opposite Page, Top:

ROW 1:

5", "Try it on the dog..." $200.00–250.00

4½", "It's an ill will wind that blows nobody good" $200.00–250.00

5", "There must be some mistake" $200.00–250.00

ROW 2:

4½", "Butting in" $200.00–250.00

5", "Do it now" $200.00–250.00

5", "Better late than never" $200.00–250.00

ROW 3:

5", "Made in Germany" $200.00–250.00

4½", "It's up to you" $200.00–250.00

5", "Ain't it hell to be poor," *Compliments of E. Hilfreich, 25 Flushing Ave., Astoria, L.I., N.Y* $200.00–250.00

ROW 4:

4½", "No vacation in this business" $200.00–250.00

4½", "This is so sudden" $200.00–250.00

4½", "Protection for infant industry" $200.00–250.00

SMOKER SETS, before 1916

Below:

ROW 1:

Ashtray, 2", Roseville Pottery Co., Zanesville, Ohio, red ink stamp $75.00–85.00

Ashtray "Fatima," 3", no mark $150.00–175.00

Indian Smoker Set, 4½" x 6½", no mark $275.00–300.00

Ashtray, 2", no mark $60.00–70.00

ROW 2:

Ashtrays, 2", no mark $60.00–70.00

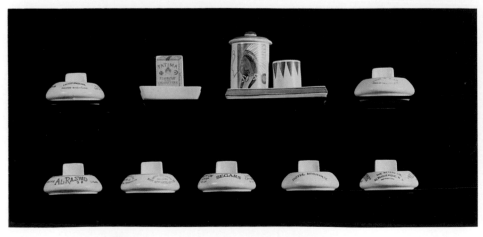

DONATELLA TEA SETS, before 1916

ROW 1: Forget–Me–Not; Creamer, 3"; Pot, 6½"; Sugar, 3½", no mark

ROW 2: Persian-type CERAMIC DESIGN; Creamer, 3"; Pot, 4½"; Sugar, 3", no mark

ROW 3: Seascape Motif; Creamer, 2½"; Pot, 4"; Sugar, 3½", no mark

ROW 4: LANDSCAPE; Creamer, 3"; Pot, 4½"; Sugar, 4", no mark

ROW 5: Gibson Girls Motif; Creamer, 3"; Pot, 4½"; Sugar, 4", no mark

ROW 1:
Set $325.00–350.00
Creamer $60.00–70.00
Sugar with Lid $70.00–80.00

ROW 2:
Set $275.00–300.00
Creamer $60.00–70.00
Sugar with Lid $70.00–80.00

ROW 3:
Set $300.00–325.00
Creamer $60.00–70.00
Sugar with Lid $70.00–80.00

ROW 4:
Set $250.00–275.00
Creamer $45.00–55.00
Sugar with Lid $55.00–65.00

ROW 5:
Set $375.00–400.00
Creamer $75.00–90.00
Sugar with Lid $100.00–110.00

ROW 1:
PERSIAN Tea Set; Creamer, 3", no mark $60.00–70.00
PERSIAN Tea Set; Teapot, 4½", no mark $150.00–175.00
PERSIAN Tea Set; Chocolate Pot, 6½", no mark...$175.00–200.00
PERSIAN Tea Set; Sugar, 4", no mark...$70.00–80.00

ROW 2:
Stylized Crocus Motif; Creamer, 3", no mark $45.00–55.00
Stylized Crocus Motif; Sugar, 4½", no mark $55.00–65.00
Good Night Candlestick, 7", no mark $450.00–500.00
Pitcher, Blue Ribbon, dainty floral decal, 5", no mark $75.00–100.00

ROW 3:
Pot/Liner, 3½", no mark..$95.00–110.00
Pot/Liner, 4", "Imperial Council Meeting, Rochester, July 11, Syrian, Cincinnati, Ohio"..................$150.00–175.00
Green Tint Pot/Liner, 4", no mark $50.00–60.00
Pot/Liner, 3½", no mark...$75.00–85.00

ROW 4:
Cherries Motif Teapot, 8½", no mark $400.00–500.00
Trivet, 6", no mark $200.00–225.00
Pitcher, floral decal, 8", no mark $200.00–225.00

GOLD TRACED and DECORATED AND GOLD TRACED, before 1916

Above:

Candlestick, 9", no mark $100.00–125.00
Candlestick, 9", no mark $125.00–150.00
Candlestick, 4", "More light goeth," mark shown above $110.00–135.00
Candlestick, 9", no mark $150.00–175.00
Candlestick, 8½", no mark $150.00–175.00

DUTCH, before 1916

ROW 1:   *Below:*
Mug, 4", no mark $100.00–125.00
Pitcher, 7½", no mark $175.00–225.00
Teapot, 4½", no mark $150.00–175.00

ROW 2:
Pin Tray, 4", no mark $65.00–75.00
Teapot, 6½", no mark $300.00–350.00
Toothbrush Holder, 4", no mark $75.00–85.00

DUTCH, before 1916

ROW 1: Creamer, 1½", no mark $75.00–85.00
Teapot, 4", no mark $125.00–150.00
Sugar, 3", no mark...$75.00–85.00
ROW 2: Soap Dish with lid (shown in stand), 3", no mark...$125.00–150.00
Milk Pitcher, 4½", no mark..$125.00–150.00
Tumbler, 4", no mark...$125.00–150.00
Tumbler, 4", no mark...$100.00–125.00
ROW 3: Humidor, 6", "Compliments of Hotel Olympia, Boston, Massachusetts" $200.00–250.00
Plate, 11", no mark..$100.00–125.00
Creamer, 3", no mark $60.00–75.00
Teapot, 7", unusual squeezebag trim $200.00–250.00
ROW 4: Combinet, 10½", no mark...$225.00–275.00
Childs Potty, 5½", no mark...$200.00–250.00
Tankard, 11½", no mark...$125.00–150.00

ROW 1: Mug, 5", "F O E, Liberty, Truth, Justice, Equality," no mark $110.00–135.00
Mug, 5", "Our Choice, 1908," no mark $225.00–275.00
Mug, 5", "Should Auld Acquaintance Be Forgot," #3 ....$250.00–275.00
Mug, 5", "F O E," no mark $100.00–125.00
ROW 2: LANDSCAPE Custard cup, 2½", no mark $50.00–60.00
LANDSCAPE Tumbler, 4", no mark...$100.00–125.00
Jardiniere/Liner, 4", no mark $85.00–95.00
Jardiniere/Liner, 3½", no mark $85.00–95.00
Mug, 3½", "Susan Swartz, 3-17-28," hand painted, no mark $200.00–250.00
ROW 3: Pitcher, 6", Roseville Potter Co., Zanesville, Ohio, red ink stamp $225.00–275.00
Coffeepot with hunt scene decal, 10", brown glazed inside $400.00–500.00
CERAMIC DESIGN Teapot, 9", no mark $300.00–400.00
ROW 4: Indian decal Mug, 5", no mark $150.00–175.00
Tankard, 11½", no mark $300.00–350.00
Mug, 5", no mark $150.00–175.00
Mug, 5", "International China, Masonic Temple, Chicago" red ink stamp $150.00–175.00
Tankard, 11½", "Loyal Order of Moose, Howdy Pap" $225.00–275.00
Mug, 5", no mark $100.00–125.00

STEIN SETS, before 1916

ROW 1: Mug, 5", floral decal, no mark $100.00–125.00

Mug, 5", Wm. Jennings Bryant, no mark..$225.00–275.00

Mug, 5", strawberry decal, no mark $100.00–125.00

ROW 2: Mugs, 5", Knights of Pythias, various scenes...$175.00–200.00

ROW 3: Mug, 5", "Englewood Commandery," No. 59 — K.T., 1000 members, Sept. 11th, 1915,

J.A. Lozier," Roseville Pottery Co., Zanesville, Ohio, red ink stamp............................$125.00–175.00

Mug, 5", Quaker Men Motif, no mark $150.00–175.00

Tankard, 12", no mark $250.00–300.00

Tankard, 12", Elk, no mark $175.00–225.00

Mug, 5", no mark $125.00–150.00

Mug, 5", Shrine, "Osman Temple, Feb. 14, 1916, no mark $150.00–175.00

ROW 4: Tankard, 12", "F O E, Liberty, Truth, Justice, Equality"...$175.00–225.00

Tankard, 12", K O P, "Friendship," no mark $400.00–450.00

Tankard, 11½", carnation decal, no mark..$225.00–275.00

Tankard, 10½", Indian decal, no mark..$300.00–350.00

Tankard, 10½", "F O E," no mark $250.00–300.00

Watch Fob, 1¾" across, "Y" in center signifies Y-Bridge in Zanesville, marked in red ink: Roseville Pottery, Zanesville, Ohio.
$400.00–500.00

ROW 1:
HOLLY Tumbler, 4", no mark $200.00–250.00
MEDALLION Pitcher, 3½", no mark $75.00–85.00
MEDALLION Creamer, 3", no mark $75.00–85.00
Creamer, Greek Key design, 3½", no mark $75.00–85.00
Quaker Children decoration, 2", no mark $100.00–125.00

ROW 2:
Toothbrush Holder, 5", Lily of the Valley decal, no mark..$150.00–175.00
Mug, 5", Wild Rose decal no mark $100.00–125.00
Mug, 5", Poppy decal, no mark..$100.00–125.00
Mug, 5", Mum decal, no mark $100.00–125.00

ROW 3:
Dog Dish, 3" x 8½", Rv ink stamp over glaze, probably later issue.......................................$150.00–175.00
Dog Dish, 2" x 5½", same mark, green with ivory lining $125.00–150.00

ROW 1:

Ring Tree, 3½", Forget–Me–Not, no mark...$85.00–95.00

Pin Box, 4", yellow ribbon with dainty floral decal, no mark...$175.00–225.00

Dresser Tray, 10", no mark $150.00–175.00

Candlesticks, 2", no mark ....*each $100.00–125.00*

ROW 2:

Pitcher, 7", decal decoration, no mark..$200.00–250.00

Spittoon, 10", Rose decal, no mark..$400.00–450.00

2 pc. Flower Arranger, 2", CERAMIC DESIGN, no mark..$75.00–85.00

2 pc. Flower Arranger, 2", no mark...$75.00–85.00

ROW 3:

Tankard, 12", no mark $225.00–275.00

Mug, 5", "International China Co, Masonic Temple, Chicago" in red ink $150.00–175.00

Tankard, 11½", no mark...$300.00–350.00

Mug, 5", no mark..$150.00–175.00

Tankard, 11½", Cherry decal, no mark $250.00–275.00

OLD IVORY, IVORY TINT, before 1916

Opposite Page, Top:

ROW 1:

Planter, 4", no mark $75.00–85.00
Humidor, 6", no mark $225.00–275.00
Double Bud Vase, 5" x 6½", no mark $100.00–125.00

ROW 2:

Jardiniere/Liner, 8", #513 ....$250.00–300.00
Tankard, 13½", no mark $300.00–350.00
Jardiniere, 9", no mark $275.00–325.00

Below Left:

Comport, 9", no mark $150.00–200.00
Pot, 3½", no mark $95.00–110.00

Opposite Page, Center:

Persian-type CERAMIC DESIGN Pot, 8", no mark $175.00–225.00
Plate with Nude, 8", no mark $450.00–550.00
LANDSCAPE Coffeepot, 10", no mark $400.00–450.00

HOLLY, before 1916

Opposite Page, Bottom:

Candlestick, 7", no mark $400.00–500.00
Teapot, 4½", no mark $300.00–350.00
Creamer, 3", no mark $175.00–200.00
Reverse side of candlestick $400.00–500.00

FORGET–ME–NOT, before 1916

Below Right:

Sugar, 3", no mark $100.00–125.00
Creamer, 1½", no mark $100.00–125.00

PERSIAN, 1916

Above: Jardiniere, 5", marked in red ink, Roseville Pottery, Zanesville, Ohio $150.00–175.00
Hanging Basket, 9", no mark $225.00–250.00
Jardiniere, 8", no mark $225.00–250.00

Below: Jardiniere, 6½", marked in red ink, Roseville Pottery, Zanesville, Ohio, #462–7 incised $125.00–150.00
Candlestick, 8½", no mark $125.00–150.00
Jardiniere, 5", no mark $125.00–150.00

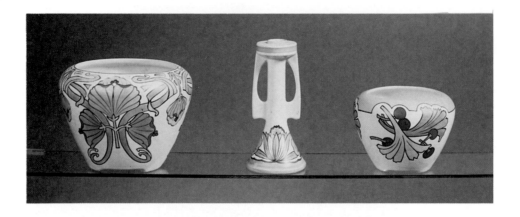

CERAMIC DESIGN, before 1916

Below: Tumblers, 4", no mark...$100.00–125.00
Pitcher, 6½", no mark $200.00–250.00

ROW 1:   Spittoon, 5", no mark $100.00–125.00
         Gold Traced Spittoon, 5", no mark..................$175.00–200.00
         Fern Trail Spittoon, 5", no mark $125.00–150.00
ROW 2:   MERCIAN Jardiniere, 8", mark at right $500.00–600.00
         OLD IVORY Jardiniere, 8", no mark.................$150.00–200.00
ROW 3:   DECORATED MATT Jardiniere, 9", (C S) $550.00–650.00
         DECORATED MATT Jardiniere, 8", (H R) $550.00–650.00

THE ROSEVILLE POTTERY Co
-MERCIAN-
545-8

BLENDED GLAZE, 1900s

Jardiniere, base diameter, 4¼", Pea
Pod embossing, no mark,
$50.00–75.00
Jardiniere and Pedestal, 12" overall,
Pine Cone decoration,
$175.00–225.00
Jardiniere, 5½", base diameter,
no mark, $85.00–95.00

VENETIAN, early 1900s

Bake Pan, 7", Venetian Imp.
$50.00–60.00
Pudding Crock, fire proof Venetian
$40.00–50.00
Bake Pan, 9", no mark
$55.00–65.00

ROW 1:
IDEAL Pitcher, 6½", Cobalt
$100.00–125.00
Bowl, orange band, 5½" x 9½", Rv
ink stamp, *$60.00–70.00*
IDEAL Pitcher, 6½", rose
$100.00–125.00

ROW 2:
Pitcher, 7½", no mark
$75.00–100.00
Pitcher, 7½", grey band,
Rv ink stamp, *$85.00–95.00*
Pitcher, 6", Rv ink stamp
$75.00–85.00

ROW 1:
Bake Pan, 3" x 10", orange band, Rv
ink stamp under glaze
$75.00–85.00
Pitcher, 8", blue band, same mark
$95.00–120.00

ROW 2:
Mug, 3½", Rv ink stamp
$60.00–70.00
Mug, 4", same mark
$60.00–70.00
Mug, 5", same mark
$60.00–70.00
Mug, 6", same mark
$75.00–85.00
Pitcher, 7½", same mark
$95.00–120.00

JUVENILE, from before 1916 through mid 1930s

ROW 1: Nursery Rhyme motif; Sugar, 3", no mark $125.00–150.00

Nursery Rhyme motif; Pot, 6", no mark $250.00–275.00

Nursery Rhyme motif; Creamer, 3", no mark $125.00–150.00

ROW 2: SANTA CLAUS Creamer, 3½", Rv ink stamp...$350.00–400.00

Rolled edge Plate, 8", Rv ink stamp...$500.00–600.00

Cup, 2"; Saucer, 5", Rv ink stamp...$450.00–500.00

ROW 3: RABBIT Mug, 3", Rv ink stamp $125.00–150.00

Rolled edge Plate, 8", Rv ink stamp...$175.00–200.00

Egg Cup, 4", Rv ink stamp...$200.00–250.00

ROW 4: PIG Plate, 8", Rv ink stamp $300.00–350.00

Creamer, 4", Rv ink stamp...$300.00–350.00

ROOSTER Plate, 8", series of numbers indicating an experimental...$400.00–500.00

ROW 5: FANCY CAT Divided Plate, 8½", Rv ink stamp...$450.00–500.00

Rolled edge Plate, 8", Rv ink stamp...$350.00–400.00

Plate, 8", Rv ink stamp...$350.00–400.00

Mug, 3", Rv ink stamp $350.00–400.00

JUVENILE

ROW 1:
FAT PUPPY Mug, 3½", no mark, green band....$200.00–250.00
Pitcher, 3½", no mark..............................$225.00–275.00
Plate, 7", no mark $250.00–300.00
Creamer, 3½", no mark $225.00–275.00
Bowl, 4½", no mark $200.00–250.00

ROW 2:
DUCK WITH BOOTS Creamer, 3"; hi-gloss;
   no mark; orange band.........................$125.00–150.00
Bowl, 5", no mark $150.00–175.00
CHICKS rolled edge Plate, 8"; hi-gloss;
   no mark; green band...........................$150.00–175.00
Bowl, 6"; hi-gloss; Rv ink stamp.................$125.00–150.00
Creamer, 3"; matt glaze, no mark $150.00–175.00

ROW 3:
Custard, 2½", no mark $125.00–175.00
Creamer, 3", no mark.............................$115.00–140.00
Small rolled edge Plate, 7", no mark.............$125.00–150.00
Pitcher, 3", no mark.............................$125.00–150.00
Bowl, 4½", no mark $125.00–150.00
Cup, 2"; Saucer, 5½", no mark $150.00–175.00

ROW 4:
Baby's Plate, 8", no mark $125.00–150.00
Egg Cup, 3½", no mark $200.00–250.00
Cake Plate, 9½", no mark $200.00–250.00
Pudding Dish, 3½", no mark......................$125.00–150.00
Plate, 7", no mark $100.00–125.00

JUVENILE

ROW 1:
BEAR Creamer, 4", no mark, green bands ...$250.00–300.00
Bowl, 6", no mark $250.00–300.00
Mug, 3½", no mark.......................................$250.00–300.00

ROW 2:
DUCK Cup, 2"; saucer, 5½", no mark,
   green bands $250.00–300.00
Teapot, 4", no mark......................................$400.00–450.00
Sugar, 3", no mark $150.00–175.00

ROW 3:
Mug, 3½", no mark.......................................$200.00–250.00
Plate, 7", no mark $175.00–225.00
Creamer, 4", no mark....................................$200.00–250.00
Custard, 2½", no mark $150.00–200.00

ROW 4:
SITTING RABBIT Custard, 2½", no mark,
   green bands $125.00–150.00
B & M set, Pitcher, 3", no mark....................$125.00–150.00
B & M set, Bowl, 4½",..................................$100.00–125.00
Creamer, 3½", no mark $125.00–150.00
Cup, 2", saucer, 5", no mark $150.00–200.00
Pudding Dish, 1½" x 3½" $125.00–150.00

ROW 5:
Egg Cup, 3", no mark $300.00–350.00
Baby's Plate, 7", no mark............................$125.00–150.00
Baby's Plate, 8", no mark............................$125.00–150.00
Plate, 7", no mark $125.00–150.00
Egg Cup, 3½", Rv ink stamp $200.00–250.00

JUVENILE

ROW 1:
Creamer, 3", no mark
$125.00–150.00
Teapot, 5", #8
$300.00–350.00
Sugar, 4", no mark
$125.00–150.00

NURSERY

ROWS 2 & 3:
Rolled edge Plates, 8", no mark
$175.00–225.00 ea.

RABBIT Pitcher, 7½", no mark
$500.00–600.00
Bowl, 10½, no mark
$500.00–600.00

ROSEVILLE POTTERY INC.
ZANESVILLE, OHIO

No. 1 JUVENILE SET

Three Piece Set Contains:

No. 1 — 3" Mug — Blue band with Duck decoration

No. 2 — 6" Bowl — Pink band with Dog decoration

No. 3 — 7" Plate — Green band with Rabbit decoration

Packed in attractive gift box

WHOLESALE PRICE

$2.50 PER SET
(Box Included)

F.O.B. Zanesville

749

JUVENILE

ROW 1:
DOG, 2-handled Mug, 3", Rv ink stamp *$150.00–175.00*
Rolled edge Plate, 8", Rv ink stamp.............*$125.00–150.00*
Cup, 2"; Saucer, 5", Rv ink stamp................*$175.00–200.00*
Plate, 8", Rv ink stamp..................................*$125.00–150.00*
Creamer, 3½", Rv ink stamp.........................*$125.00–150.00*

ROW 2:
DUCK WITH HAT Creamer, 3½",
  Rv ink stamp...*$100.00–125.00*
Cup, 2"; Saucer, 3", Rv ink stamp.................*$150.00–175.00*
Rolled edge Plate, 8", Rv ink stamp.............*$125.00–150.00*
Plate, 8", Rv ink stamp..................................*$125.00–150.00*
2-handled Mug, 3", Rv ink stamp *$100.00–125.00*
Mug, 3", Rv ink stamp *$100.00–125.00*

ROW 3:
SUNBONNET GIRL Creamer, 3½",
  Rv ink stamp...*$100.00–125.00*
Cup, 2"; Saucer, 3", Rv ink stamp................*$150.00–200.00*
Rolled edge Plate, 8", Rv ink stamp.............*$125.00–175.00*
Plate, 8", Rv ink stamp..................................*$125.00–175.00*
Egg Cup, 4", Rv ink stamp...........................*$200.00–250.00*
2-handled Mug, 3", Rv ink stamp *$150.00–175.00*

ROW 4:
Experimental Mug, 3"; Vitro #1237..............*$250.00–300.00*
Boxed Set *$700.00–800.00*
Potty, 3" x 6", no mark *$250.00–300.00*
(add $100.00 for lid)

SYNOPSIS OF COMPANY PRICE LIST, 1916

In the Roseville files at the Ohio Historical Society, there is a price list dated July, 1916. It is 24 pages long, and full of both enlightening facts and puzzling references.

Alphabetically beginning with "Art," the index refers us to a page entitled "Special Art Assortment." Listed are such familiar things as Matt Green Gates, Goodnight Candlesticks, Dutch Tea Pots, etc. Sylvan flower vases are listed, two years earlier than we once thought they were produced. "Green Tint" gates are offered . . . and "Coral" ferns and "Cremona" tobacco jars hint at lines as yet unidentified. (Another page of the catalogue is devoted entirely to "Cremona" — tankard sets, smoker sets, dresser sets and tea sets are listed — and that, along with the fact that during these middle teen years creamware was extremely popular, would strongly suggest that this Cremona was a creamware line. The more familiar Cremona line would not be produced for nearly a dozen more years!)

Birds and Bowls were offered in Red, Blue, Black, Yellow, Carnelian and Matt White . . . and some birds were available decorated by hand. Bowls were listed in 6", 8", 10", 12" and 14" sizes. Evidently a popular combination, black bowls were paired with yellow birds, yellow bowls with black birds — sixteen sizes and combinations, all black and yellow, with prices ranging from $10.50 to $22.00 per dozen! Bouquet Holders in the shapes of a frog, turtle, fish and toad were mentioned, finished in the same colors.

Under "Baby Plates" is a nursery assortment of familiar items — bread and milk sets, custards, tea pots, etc — but the bottom half of the page is devoted to the "Holly" line, and reveals that creamers, childrens mugs, fern dishes, ash trays, dresser sets, smoker sets were produced, in addition to those items we were able to photograph for the color plates.

"Lily of the Valley" was the name of a 12 pc. Toilet set — "Osiris" was another. "Jeanette" was offered in cuspidor #909 shape, and later in jardinieres and pedestals and umbrella stands.

"Hoster Flagon Steins" in 8 oz., 10 oz., and 12 oz. sizes were advertised as having a "White lining." Bedroom sets consisting of candlesticks, match receiver, pitcher, and tray, came with either orange or blue bands — there are examples of these in the color plates.

A notation concerning the company policy for pricing tea sets and individual pieces seems sound yet today: Teapot — ½ price entire set; Sugar bowl — ⅓ price entire set; creamer — ½ price of sugar bowl.

And yes, wall pocket collectors, a Tourist wall pocket is listed — 10" X 5" at $9.00 per dozen! Tourist window boxes are priced at $3.00 for a 6½" X 11", and $4.50 each for 8" X 14". An 8½" X 16" size was offered at $6.00.

The Blended Glaze and Matt Green ware were popular finishes, as were Carnelian, Black, Yellow, and Blue Rosecraft — as well as one referred to simply as "Red." "Red" jardinieres and pedestals in 29" and 33" heights were priced at $4.50 and $7.50 each . . . these were also offered in the Rosecraft glazes!

So, though informative and exciting, the 1916 price list leaves us with only vague suggestions of a line called "Coral" . . . a "Cremona" . . . "Osiris" . . . a puzzling red glaze . . . birds and bowls. Perhaps in the future, further research will give us these answers.

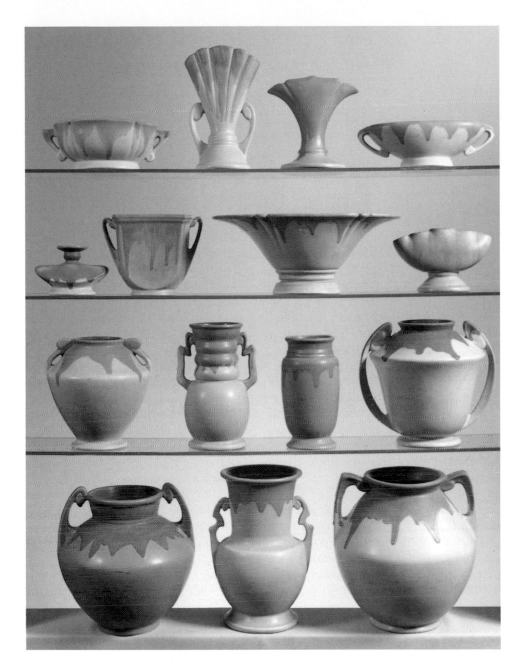

CARNELIAN I, 1910–15

ROW 1:
Bowl/Frog, 3" x 8½", small black paper label $80.00–90.00
Vase, 8", Rv ink stamp $85.00–95.00
Fan Vase, 6", Rv ink stamp $60.00–70.00
Bowl, 3" x 9", Rv ink stamp $80.00–90.00

ROW 2:
Candleholder/Frog, 3½", Rv ink stamp $60.00–70.00
Pillow Vase, 5", Rv ink stamp $80.00–90.00
Console, 5" x 12½", Rv ink stamp $125.00–150.00
Flower Frog, 4½", Rv ink stamp $65.00–75.00

ROW 3:
Vase, 7", no mark $100.00–125.00
Vase, 8", Rv ink stamp $95.00–115.00
Vase, 7", Rv ink stamp $90.00–100.00
Vase, 8", Rv ink stamp $125.00–150.00

ROW 4:
Vase, 9½", Rv ink stamp $150.00–200.00
Vase, 10", Rv ink stamp $150.00–200.00
Vase, 10", Rv ink stamp $150.00–200.00

PRODUCTION AFTER 1917

In 1917, the company was producing a line of utility ware "for hotels, cafes and family". Romafin was plain and undecorated, in "mahogany red with a white lining". The catalogue presented 9 pages of the ware in a wide variety of baking pans, pudding crocks, etc. Also listed was a complete line of tea pot shapes, some of which were made in a black glaze as well as the mahogany.

"Donnatella" tea sets were made in various patterns during this period; included were Ceramic, Dutch, and Landscape. The 3 pc. sets were priced at $1.25. Seven piece stein sets in the Dutch pattern sold at $3.00, others were $4.00.

Victorian Art Pottery is a seldom seen line, made from 1924-28. Simple shapes in blue-grey are usually decorated with a band of leaves and berries; or in dark brown with a band of stylized leaves and pods. However, an occasional piece in the blue-grey will be found with the stylized shoulder band; one example is shown later on. Vase shapes in a glossy yellow were also utilized as lamp bases.

By the late 20's and into the early 30's, simple, beautiful glazes were often favored over elaborate modeling. The Futura line combined the best of both the modeler's effort and the chemist's technology. Several pages were featured in the company's catalogues, and Futura collectors find still other shapes not shown — evidently added to the line at a later time. One of these, a window box in an elegant Art Deco style, glazed in the lovely carmel and turquoise that was often used within the line, is very suggestive of a line that was introduced sometime around 1930 . . . Artcraft. Examples of this lovely line are shown in the color plates, along with the original company label which made its identification official.

In 1926, Russell T. Young, (son of George Young, founder of the Roseville Pottery) who was at that time President of the Company) built a home at 1327 Blue Avenue in Zanesville. The Tudor-manor style structure was designed by Insco Associates of Columbus, O., and constructed by The Dunzweiler Company. One of the specially designed ceramic tile radiator covers from the home is shown in the color plates. It is from a set designed by Frank Ferrell, and made by George Krause.

From as early at 1917, lines that featured a floral pattern were popular sellers. Mock Orange in 1950 was the last of many. By the late 1940's, in an attempt to revive lagging sales, several lines were produced in a high gloss glaze — however, all met with limited success. Two of these lines were Capri, only recently officially named, and Artwood, which was incorrectly identified in Volume I as part of the Wincraft line. Examples of both are shown later.

Our study has only fortified our appreciation . . . for the integrity of the man who founded the Roseville Pottery . . . for those that followed who carried on in the same irreproachable manner . . . and for the pride taken in their work by the artists and craftsmen who were so dedicated to their art.

CARNELIAN II, 1915

Above Right:

ROW 1:

Vase, 5", no mark $175.00–200.00
Vase, 7", no mark $175.00–200.00
Planter, 3" x 8", small black paper label $95.00–120.00

ROW 2:

Vase, 8", no mark $225.00–275.00
Vase, 6", black paper label $225.00–275.00
Vase, 8", no mark $225.00–275.00

ROW 3:

Vase, 7", Rv ink stamp and black paper label $150.00–175.00
Ewer, 12½", no mark $500.00–600.00
Vase, 10", no mark $150.00–175.00
Vase, 8", no mark $175.00–200.00

CARNELIAN II, 1915

ROW 1:
Vase, 12", no mark
$450.00–550.00
Vase, 15", no mark
$700.00–800.00
Vase, 12", no mark
$450.00–550.00

ROW 2:
Vase, 12", no mark
$600.00–700.00
Lamp Base, 8", no mark
$350.00–400.00
Vase, 14", small black paper label
$600.00–700.00

Below:
Vase, 18½", no mark
$1,000.00–1,200.00
Vase, 14½", no mark
$650.00–750.00

In Volume I, on page 151, you will find a catalogue reprint showing many of these unusual Carnelian shapes, with the year 1915 penciled in. When the first book was done, no examples of this type had been found, and the glaze treatment was impossible to determine from the catalogue page alone. However, these examples have glazes identical to the Carnelian on the previous page — the type which collectors prefer to call Carnelian II.

CARNELIAN II, 1915

ROW 1:

Vase, 8", no mark $175.00–225.00
Basket, 4" x 10", Rv ink stamp and small black paper label $200.00–300.00
Vase, 7", no mark $150.00–175.00

ROW 2:

Bowl, 3" x 8", no mark $75.00–100.00
Bowl, 5" x 12½", Rv ink stamp $250.00–300.00
Fan Vase, 6½", Rv ink stamp $75.00–100.00

ROW 3:

Bowl, 4" x 10", Rv ink stamp $200.00–250.00
Bowl, 4" x 15", no mark $400.00–450.00

ROW 4:

Vase, 9", Silver Paper label $200.00–250.00
Vase, 9", no mark $200.00–250.00
Vase, 8", no mark $150.00–200.00
Frog, 4" x 6", Rv ink stamp $100.00–150.00

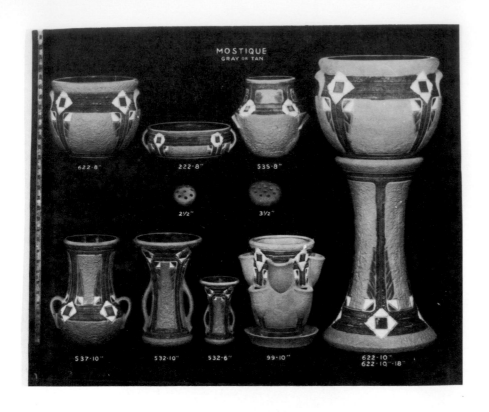

MOSTIQUE
GRAY or TAN

622·8"   222·8"   535·8"

2½"   3½"

537·10"   532·10"   532·6"   99·10"   622·10"
622·10"·18"

Below:

Jardiniere, 10"
$150.00–200.00
Metal Stand, 38"
$200.00–250.00

740   N·150   160
38½ overall   38½ overall   38½ in overall

MOSTIQUE, 1915

ROW 1:

Hanging Basket, 7", no mark $150.00–225.00
Bowl, 7", no mark $65.00–75.00
Bowl, 7", no mark $65.00–75.00
Bowl, 5½", no mark $65.00–75.00

ROW 2:

Bowl, 9½", no mark $85.00–95.00
Comport, 7", no mark $125.00–150.00
Bowl, 9", no mark $125.00–150.00

ROW 3:

Vase, 10", no mark $200.00–225.00
Vase, 12", no mark $250.00–300.00
Jardiniere, 8", no mark $125.00–150.00
Vase, 6", no mark $90.00–100.00

ROSECRAFT PANEL, 1920

ROW 1:
Vase, 6", Rv ink stamp
$100.00–125.00
Covered Jar, 10", small Rv ink stamp
$450.00–550.00
Bowl Vase, 4", Rv ink stamp
$100.00–125.00

ROW 2:
Lamp Base, 10", silver paper label, X1F8
$700.00–800.00
Window Box, 6" x 12", Rv ink stamp
$250.00–300.00
Vase, 10", Rv ink stamp
$250.00–275.00

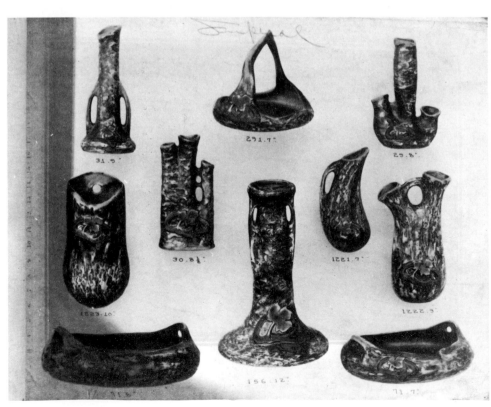

IMPERIAL I, 1916

ROW 1:

Basket, 9", #7 ....$100.00–125.00

Basket, 10", #8 ....$125.00–150.00

Basket, 10", #9 ....$125.00–150.00

Vase, 8", no mark $100.00–125.00

ROW 2:

Vase, 10", no mark $150.00–200.00

Comport, 6½", no mark..$100.00–135.00

Vase, 8", no mark $125.00–175.00

ROW 3:

Vase, 10", no mark $125.00–175.00

Planter, 14" x 16", no mark..$100.00–150.00

Vase, 12", no mark $125.00–175.00

DONATELLO, 1915

ROW 1:
Powder Jar, 2" x 5", no mark
$250.00–300.00
Vase, 6", no mark
$150.00–175.00
Double Bud Vase, 7", no mark
$200.00–250.00
Incense Burner, 3½", no mark
$300.00–350.00

ROW 2:
Vase, 8½", no mark, unusual grey
coloring, $175.00–225.00
Vase, 12", no mark
$175.00–200.00
Vase, 9½", no mark
$150.00–175.00
Plate, 8", no mark
$250.00–300.00

This metal stencil measures 16½" x 3" and was used to
letter packing crates.
$200.00–300.00

Below it is a light sconce, 18" x 6", made by the Roseville
Pottery for the Rogge Hotel in Zanesville, now demolished.
$600.00–700.00

DONATELLO, 1915

ROW 1:
Bowl, 6", no mark $55.00–65.00
Ashtray, 3", no mark $125.00–150.00
Hanging Basket, 7", no mark $175.00–200.00
Ashtray, 3", Rv ink stamp............................$125.00–150.00
Ashtray, 2", no mark $150.00–175.00

ROW 2:
Rolled edge Bowl, 9½", no mark...................$90.00–120.00
Bowl, 8½" x 3½", Rv ink stamp, #238/7.........$90.00–120.00
Bowl, 8" x 3", no mark $90.00–120.00

ROW 3:
Cuspidor, 5½", no mark...............................$200.00–250.00
Jardiniere, 6", no mark $125.00–150.00
Comport, 5", no mark.....................................$75.00–100.00
Candlestick, 6½", no mark $125.00–150.00

ROW 4:
Vase, 8", no mark $65.00–75.00
Vase, 10", no mark $100.00–125.00
Vase, 12", no mark $175.00–200.00
Comport, 9½", Impressed Donatello seal $150.00–175.00
Basket, 7½", Impressed Donatello seal $200.00–250.00

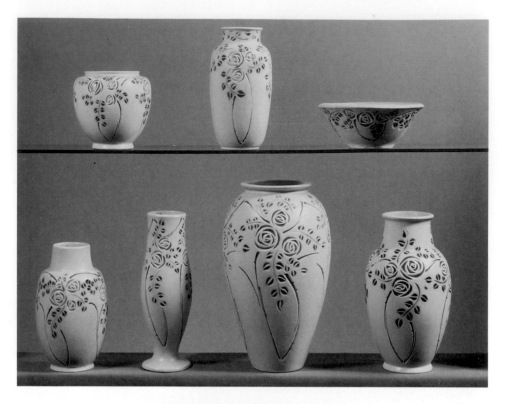

VELMOSS SCROLL, 1916

ROW 1:
Vase, 5", no mark $125.00–150.00
Vase, 8", no mark $125.00–175.00
Bowl, 3", C7, no mark $75.00–100.00

ROW 2:
Vase, 8", no mark $125.00–150.00
Vase, 10", no mark $175.00–225.00
Vase, 12", no mark $250.00–300.00
Vase, 10", no mark $150.00–200.00

ROZANE, 1917

ROW 1:
Bowl, 3", Roseville Rozane Pottery, black ink stamp;
    green glaze $50.00–75.00
Comport, 8", no mark...................................$75.00–125.00
Vase, 6½", Rozane black ink stamp;
    pink glaze $50.00–75.00

ROW 2:
Urn, 6½", Rozane black ink stamp.................$75.00–100.00
Footed Bowl, 5", Rozane black ink stamp....$125.00–175.00
Bowl, 3½", no mark...$65.00–75.00

ROW 3:
Bowl, 5", Rozane black ink stamp $100.00–125.00
Comport, 6½", no mark $100.00–125.00
Bowl, 4½", no mark.......................................$90.00–115.00

ROW 4:
Basket, 11", Rozane ink stamp; blue glaze...$150.00–175.00
Vase, 8", Rozane ink stamp...............................$65.00–90.00
Vase, 10", Rozane ink stamp, green glaze $90.00–110.00
Vase, 10", Rozane ink stamp, yellow glaze $90.00–110.00
Vase, 8", no mark $75.00–90.00

Obviously from the Rosecraft era, this recently discovered line of ware has no official name. It may have been an alternate glaze treatment within the Rosecraft line (reprint shown above for comparison), or it may have had its own identity. Collectors tend to refer to is most often as Rosecraft Blended.
(Shown at bottom of opposite page.)

AZURINE, ORCHID, and TURQUOISE

Pair of Bud Vases, 10", black paper label, turquoise glaze
$100.00–150.00
Console Bowl, 12½", no mark, turquoise glaze
$75.00–100.00

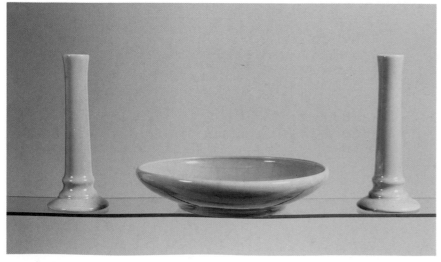

LOMBARDY, 1924

Left:
Jardiniere, 6½", black paper label $150.00–200.00
Vase, 6", no mark......................................$150.00–200.00

AZURINE, ORCHID, and TURQUOISE, 1920

Below:
Double Bud Vase, 5" x 8", no mark $55.00–75.00
Vase, 10", no mark...................................$125.00–150.00
Vase, 8", no mark.....................................$75.00–100.00

ROSECRAFT BLENDED, late teens

Below:
ROW 1:
Vase, 6", no mark........................*$75.00–85.00*
Window Box, 5" x 8", with
  separate Frog *$75.00–100.00*
Jardiniere, 4", no mark *$65.00–75.00*
Bud Vase, #36–6 ....*$65.00–75.00*

ROW 2:
Vase, 10", #35...........................*$100.00–125.00*
Vase, 8", no mark......................*$125.00–150.00*
Vase, 12½", no mark *$125.00–150.00*

ROSECRAFT BLACK and COLORS, 1916

ROW 1:
Comport, 4" x 11", no mark $100.00–125.00
ROW 2:
Bowl, 3" x 8", no mark $65.00–75.00
Double Bud Vase, 5", no mark $85.00–95.00
Bowl/Frog, 2" x 8½", small silver paper label $50.00–75.00
ROW 3:
Bowl, 5", Rv ink stamp, blue glaze $100.00–125.00
Ginger Jar, 8", small paper label..$200.00–250.00
Bud Base, 8", Rv ink stamp, yellow glaze...$65.00–75.00
Flower Pot, 4½", no mark, yellow glaze $125.00–150.00
ROW 4:
Vase, 10", Rv ink stamp, blue glaze $150.00–200.00
Vase, 13½", small silver paper label $200.00–225.00
Vase, 10", no mark $150.00–175.00
Vase, 9", small silver paper label..$150.00–175.00

ROSECRAFT VINTAGE, 1924

ROW 1:
Bowl, 3", Rv ink stamp
$100.00–125.00
Vase, 6", Rv ink stamp
$150.00–175.00
Vase, 4", no mark
$100.00–125.00

ROW 2:
Vase, 8½", Rv ink stamp
$150.00–175.00
Window Box, 6" x 11½",
Rv ink stamp, *$225.00–275.00*
Vase, 12", small Rv ink stamp
$250.00–300.00

ROSECRAFT HEXAGON, 1924

ROW 1:
Vase, 6", Rv ink stamp
$200.00–225.00
Vase, 5", Rv ink stamp
$175.00–200.00
Vase, 5", Blue hi-gloss glaze, Rv
ink stamp, *$225.00–250.00*
Vase, 4", Rv ink stamp
$150.00–175.00
Bowl, 7½", Rv ink stamp
$150.00–175.00

ROW 2:
Candlestick, 8", Rv ink stamp
$200.00–250.00
Vase, 8", Rv ink stamp
$250.00–300.00
Double Bud Vase, 5", small Rv ink
stamp, *$200.00–250.00*
Vase, 8", small Rv ink stamp
$250.00–300.00
Candlestick, 8", Rv ink stamp
$200.00–250.00

LUSTRE, 1921

ROW 1:
Basket, 10", no mark
$100.00–150.00
Basket, 6", no mark
$125.00–150.00

ROW 2:
Bowl, 5", no mark
$35.00–45.00
Vase, 12", small black paper label
$75.00–85.00
Candlestick, 10", Rv impressed
$75.00–85.00
Candlestick, 5½", Rv impressed
$65.00–75.00

Vase, 12", Rv impressed
$175.00–200.00
Basket, 6½", Rv impressed and small black paper label
$100.00–125.00

MATT COLOR, late 1920s

Bowl, 3", #15, silver paper label
$60.00–70.00
Vase, 4", small silver paper label
$60.00–70.00
Bowl, 4", no mark, *$60.00–70.00*
Vase, 4", small silver paper label
$60.00–70.00
Pot, 4", small black paper label
$60.00–70.00

IMPERIAL II, 1924

Vase, 9", no mark
$300.00–350.00
Vase, 10", #477 in red crayon
$450.00–500.00
Vase, 8", black paper label
$300.00–350.00
Vase, 8", #473 in red crayon
$350.00–400.00

IMPERIAL II, 1924

ROW 1:
Bowl, 4½", no mark $200.00–250.00
Vase, 5½", no mark $175.00–200.00
Vase, 7", no mark...................$250.00–300.00
Vase, 4½", no mark $150.00–200.00
Vase, 6", no mark...................$300.00–350.00

ROW 2:
Bowl, 4½", no mark $300.00–350.00
Vase, 5", no mark...................$200.00–225.00
Bowl, 5" x 9", no mark............$400.00–450.00
Vase, 5", black paper label $250.00–300.00

ROW 3:
Vase, 7", black paper label $300.00–350.00
Vase, 4", no mark...................$150.00–200.00
Bowl, 5" x 12½", no mark $375.00–425.00
Vase, 7", no mark...................$400.00–450.00

ROW 4:
Vase, 8½", no mark $450.00–500.00
Vase, 8", no mark...................$325.00–375.00
Vase, 11", no mark..................$500.00–600.00
Vase, 8½", no mark $450.00–500.00

DOGWOOD I, 1918

ROW 1:
Vase, 7", Rv ink stamp
$125.00–150.00
Hanging Basket, 7", no mark
$125.00–150.00
Bowl, 2½", Rv ink stamp
$50.00–75.00

ROW 2:
Bowl, 4", Rv ink stamp
$75.00–85.00
Jardiniere, 6", Rv ink stamp
$95.00–115.00
Jardiniere, 8", Rv ink stamp
$125.00–150.00

DOGWOOD II, 1928

ROW 1:
Double Bud Vase, 8", no mark
$100.00–135.00
Tub, 4" x 7", no mark
$80.00–100.00

ROW 2:
Window Box/Liner, 5½" x 13½",
no mark, *$150.00–175.00*
Vase, 14½", no mark
$350.00–400.00

ROW 1:

Vase, 6", black paper label.............................$100.00–125.00
Hanging Basket, 7½", no mark $150.00–175.00
Pillow Vase, 5" x 7", no mark $100.00–125.00

ROW 2:

Candlesticks, 3½", black paper label ....$150.00–175.00 pair
Vase, 6", no mark $125.00–175.00
Bowl Vase, 4", no mark $100.00–125.00

ROW 3:

Vase, 8", no mark $125.00–175.00
Window Box, 6" x 12½", small silver label...$150.00–200.00
Bud Vase, 8", no mark...................................$125.00–150.00

ROW 4:

Window Box, 6" x 16", takes ceramic liner,
   no mark $250.00–275.00
Window Box, 6" x 11½", takes liner, no mark..$175.00–225.00

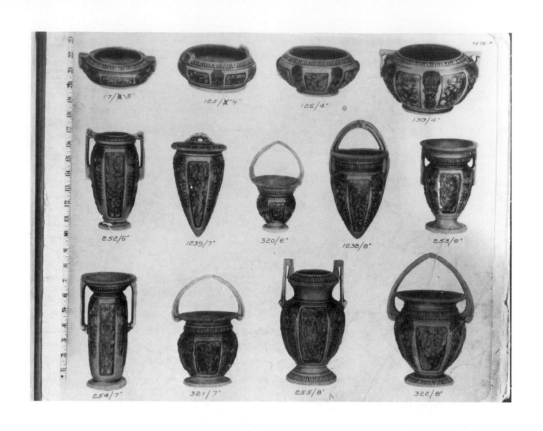

17/X·3"   125/X·4"   126/4"   130/4"

252/6"   1239/7"   320/6"   1238/8"   253/6"

254/7"   321/7"   255/8"   322/8"

FLORENTINE

1062·4"   6·4"   339·5"   602·6"   602·5"   130·4"

322·8"   321·7"   1238·7"   126·7"

252·6"

231·8"   255·8"

233·10"   232·10"   234·12"   763·20"   602·

90

FLORENTINE, 1924

ROW 1:
Hanging Basket, 9" across, Rv ink stamp.....*$125.00–175.00*
Jardiniere, 5", Rv ink stamp *$95.00–110.00*
Ashtray, 5", no mark *$85.00–95.00*
Vase, 8", black paper label...........................*$100.00–125.00*

ROW 2:
Bowl, 7", no mark *$50.00–60.00*
Bowl, 9", no mark *$65.00–75.00*
Bowl, 7", no mark *$50.00–60.00*

ROW 3:
Candlestick, 10½", Rv ink stamp *$100.00–125.00*
Candlestick, 8½", no mark *$75.00–100.00*
Lamp Base, 8", no mark................................*$300.00–350.00*
Vase, 7", Rv ink stamp...................................*$100.00–125.00*
Double Bud Vase, 4½", no mark......................*$50.00–75.00*

ROW 4:
Jardiniere, 5¾" base diameter, no mark *$150.00–200.00*
Window Box, 11½", small Rv ink stamp *$150.00–200.00*

CREMONA, 1927

Urn, 4", no mark
$125.00–150.00
Fan, 5", no mark
$100.00–125.00
Vase, 8", no mark
$150.00–175.00
Vase, 12", no mark
$200.00–250.00

VICTORIAN ART POTTERY, 1924

Opposite Page, Bottom Left:
Covered Jar, 8", Rv ink stamp, unusual glossy glaze $400.00–450.00

Opposite Page, Bottom Right:
ROW 1:
Vase, 6", no mark $200.00–250.00
Urn, 4", no mark $150.00–175.00

ROW 2:
Vase, 6", Rv ink stamp...$200.00–250.00
Vase, 8", no mark $250.00–350.00
Vase, 7", no mark $250.00–300.00

FOREST, 1920s (?)

ROW 1:
Basket, 12", no mark
$275.00–325.00
Vase, 10", no mark
$250.00–300.00
Basket, 9½", no mark
$225.00–275.00

ROW 2:
Vase, 15", #121–15
$400.00–500.00
Vase, 18", no mark
$450.00–600.00
Vase, 18", #134–18
$400.00–500.00

VICTORIAN ART POTTERY

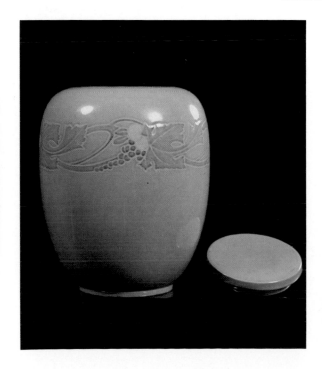

TUSCANY, 1927

ROW 1:

Vase, 4", black paper label...$85.00–95.00
Vase, 6", no mark $90.00–115.00
Flower Arranger, 5½", no mark $100.00–125.00

ROW 2:

Vase, 6", no mark $90.00–115.00
Vase, 9", no mark $150.00–175.00
Vase, 12", soft turquoise glaze $200.00–250.00

SAVONA, 1924

VOLPATO, 1918

These two lines utilize the same molds — Volpato is always ivory; Savona is salmon, blue, or lime.

ROW 1:
Covered Urn, 8", no mark $225.00–275.00

ROW 2:
Candlesticks, 9½", Rv impressed ......$250.00–275.00 pair
Vase, 12", black paper label $200.00–225.00

ROW 1:
Candlestick, 3½", no mark
$50.00–60.00
Console Bowl, 4" x 10", no mark
$100.00–125.00
Savona Candlestick, 3½"
$85.00–95.00

ROW 2:
Window Box, 2½" x 9", no mark
$45.00–55.00
Pot/Saucer, 6", no mark
$150.00–175.00
Vase, 9", no mark
$125.00–150.00
Candlestick, 10", black paper label
$100.00–125.00

NORMANDY

Hanging Basket, 7", no mark
$250.00–300.00

LA ROSE

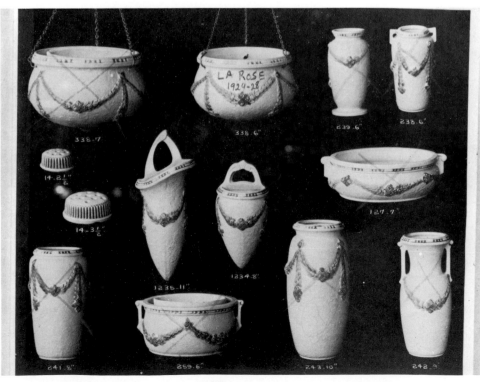

CORINTHIAN, 1923

Vase, 8½", no mark
$80.00–100.00
Jardiniere, 7", Rv ink stamp
$85.00–100.00

ROW 1:
Wall Pocket, 8", no mark
$150.00–175.00
Hanging Basket, 8", no mark
$140.00–170.00
Wall Pocket, 8½", no mark
$150.00–175.00

ROW 2:
Footed Bowl, 4½", no mark
$60.00–70.00
Vase, 6", no mark
$65.00–75.00
Vase, 7", no mark
$75.00–85.00
Bowl, 3", Rv ink stamp
$40.00–45.00

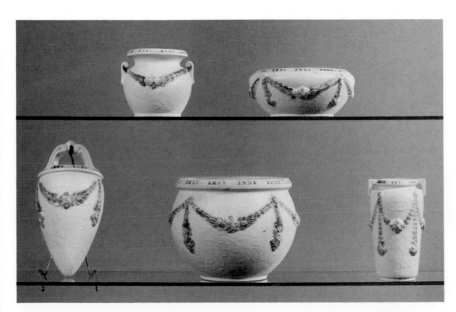

LA ROSE, 1924

ROW 1:
Vase, 4", Rv ink stamp
$95.00–110.00
Bowl, 3", Rv ink stamp
$95.00–110.00

ROW 2:
Wall Pocket, 9", no mark
$150.00–200.00
Jardiniere, 6½", Rv ink stamp
$100.00–125.00
Vase, 6", no mark
$90.00–100.00

CHERRY BLOSSOM 1932

627-5"   350-5"   627-4"

627-7"   627-6"

627-8"   627-10"   627-9"   627-10"

CHERRY BLOSSOM, 1932

Hanging Basket, 8", no mark
$400.00–500.00

FLORANE, 1920s

Bowl, 5", Rv ink stamp
$40.00–50.00
Vase, 12½", Rv ink stamp
$100.00–150.00
Basket, 8½", Rv ink stamp
$125.00–150.00
Double Bud Vase, 5", Rv ink stamp
$40.00–60.00

RUSSCO, 1930s

ROW 1:
Vase, 8", note heavy crystals, penciled notation on bottom: #61-183, over fired $150.00–175.00
Vase, 7", no mark $125.00–150.00

ROW 2:
Double Bud Vase, 8½", no mark..$100.00–125.00
Vase, 9½", no mark $125.00–150.00
Vase, 8½", no mark $125.00–150.00

ROW 3:
Vase, 7", no mark $125.00–150.00
Vase 12½", small silver paper label $200.00–250.00
Triple Cornucopia, 8" x 12½", small silver paper label..$200.00–250.00

WISTERIA, 1933

Above:
Vase, 10", silver paper label
$450.00–550.00
blue, *$700.00–900.00*
Hanging Basket, 7½", no mark
$500.00–550.00

Left:
Vase, 8½", silver paper label
$300.00–350.00
Vase, 8½", silver paper label
$350.00–450.00
Bowl Vase, 5", no mark
$250.00–350.00

JONQUIL, 1931

ROW 1:
Bowl, 3", no mark $125.00–150.00
Candlestick, 4", no mark $100.00–125.00
Bowl, 3½" x 9", no mark...............................$175.00–200.00
Vase, 4½", no mark.......................................$125.00–150.00
Vase, 4", no mark $150.00–175.00

ROW 2:
Vase, 4", no mark $125.00–150.00
Vase, 5½", no mark.......................................$150.00–175.00
Pot/Frog, 5½" (1 pc.), no mark $250.00–300.00
Vase, 4½", no mark.......................................$225.00–275.00

ROW 3:
Vase, 7", no mark $175.00–225.00
Vase, 6½", black paper label $175.00–225.00
Vase, 6½", silver paper label $225.00–275.00
Crocus Pot, 7", (1 pc.), no mark $300.00–400.00

ROW 4:
Vase, 8", small silver paper label..................$175.00–225.00
Vase, 9½", no mark.......................................$225.00–275.00
Vase, 12", no mark $500.00–600.00
Vase, 8", small black paper label..................$250.00–300.00

FUTURA, 1928

ROW 1:
Vase, 7½", no mark $450.00–500.00
Vase, 8", no mark $450.00–500.00
Vase, 7", no mark $450.00–550.00
Vase, 6", no mark $150.00–200.00
Pillow Vase, 5" x 6", black paper label $150.00–200.00

ROW 2:
Vase, 4" x 6", black paper label.......................$150.00–200.00
Vase, 3½", no mark $150.00–175.00
Fan Vase, 6", small black paper label............$175.00–200.00
Vase, 4", no mark $175.00–225.00

ROW 3:
Window Box, 5" x 15½", no mark $1,000.00–1,250.00
Candlestick, 4", small black paper label.......$125.00–150.00
Jardiniere, 6", no mark $175.00–225.00

ROW 4:
Vase, 6½", small black paper label $175.00–225.00
Vase, 5", no mark $175.00–225.00
Vase, 10", no mark $450.00–600.00
Vase, 8½", no mark $500.00–600.00
Vase, 7", no mark $150.00–200.00

"Appeal effectively to the higher aesthetic tastes" —BECKWITH

LONG AGO people of unerring taste discovered that articles of adornment have an immense value in expressing personality in the home.

How true this is of the intriguing *Futura* designs in Roseville Pottery! In the few examples given here you can catch the modernistic beauty of Futura . . . the dashing lines . . . the fearless spirit that Roseville craftsmen have so artfully given them.

In this fascinating pottery, there is an exhilarating variety to select from. There are bowls, vases, candlesticks, wall-pockets, jardinieres, hanging baskets . . . scarcely any two alike . . . delightfully tinted in harmonies of blues, grays, tans, reds and greens.

Certainly Futura lends distinction . . . creates a decorative touch superb and uncommon. And so you will want to see these shapes. They will be shown to you at leading stores, where you can make a choice for yourself, or as unusual gifts.

The abundantly illustrated booklet, "Pottery", is yours for the asking. Write for a copy. You will find it interesting.

THE ROSEVILLE POTTERY CO., *Zanesville, Ohio*

ROSEVILLE POTTERY

IF you love good pottery you will find keen moments of joy in these richly delightful, happily distinctive creations of Roseville master craftsmen.

Here are lines and curves and angles that have sprung right out of a many-sided spirit of artistry. Roseville potters live their craft and for more than a generation their handiwork has won the favor of those who appreciate charming things.

And exquisite indeed are the colors of these beautiful pieces. Subtle harmonies of pleasing tints and blending tones. Blue, gray, tan, rose, green . . . soft as the hues of twilight.

In Roseville Pottery there is a wealth of fascinating objects . . . for you to choose for yourself . . . or as a gift to someone near. There are flower bowls, vases, jars, candlesticks, wall pockets, jardinieres . . . in many sizes and shapes. You will enjoy seeing them at the leading stores, where they are on display.

The story of pottery is interestingly told in the booklet, "Pottery". . . . A free copy is awaiting you . . . Write for it

THE ROSEVILLE POTTERY COMPANY, *Zanesville, Ohio*

ROSEVILLE POTTERY

**FUTURA,
1928**

Vase, 10", no mark
$1,100.00–1,250.00
Vase, 12½", small black paper label
$800.00–1,000.00

FUTURA, 1928

ROW 1:

Vase, 5", no mark $125.00–150.00
Bowl, 2½" x 10½", silver paper label..$250.00–350.00
Vase, 6", no mark $125.00–150.00

ROW 2:

Bowl, 3½", no mark $200.00–250.00
Bowl, 3½", no mark $150.00–175.00
Bowl, 4", no mark $175.00–200.00

ROW 3:

Vase, 8", no mark $200.00–250.00
Vase, 7½", no mark $500.00–600.00
Vase, 9½", no mark $4,000.00–5,000.00
Vase, 9", no mark $650.00–750.00

ROW 4:

Vase, 9", no mark $400.00–450.00
Vase, 10", small black paper label..$400.00–450.00
Vase, 15½", small black paper label $600.00–700.00
Vase, 10", small black paper label..$450.00–550.00
Vase, 8", no mark $300.00–400.00

"Ever-varying features of the enrapturing spirit of beauty."—ANON.

THIS delightful new pottery by Roseville—*Futura*—brings into your home the charm and the exhilarating tang of the modern. There are bowls, vases and other pieces in exquisite shapes and soft colors. They make wonderfully interesting gifts. Leading stores have them.

Send for a copy of the handsomely illustrated free booklet, "Pottery"

THE ROSEVILLE POTTERY CO., ZANESVILLE, OHIO.

ROSEVILLE POTTERY

FUTURA, 1928

ROW 1:
Vase, 8", small black paper label
$175.00–225.00
Vase, 7", no mark
$500.00–600.00
Vase, 9", no mark
$250.00–300.00

ROW 2:
Vase, 9", small silver paper label
$450.00–550.00
Vase, 10", no mark
$900.00–1,000.00
Vase, 8", small silver paper label
$400.00–450.00

TOURMALINE, 1933

ROW 1:

Vase, 5½", small silver paper label $100.00–125.00
Candlesticks, 5", silver paper label ....$175.00–200.00 pair
Pillow Vase, 6", no mark $100.00–125.00
Vase, 6", small silver paper label..$100.00–125.00

ROW 2:

Vase, 4½", no mark...$90.00–100.00
Vase, 7", no mark $125.00–150.00
Vase, 6", small silver paper label..$125.00–150.00
Bowl, 8", small silver paper label $75.00–100.00

ROW 3:

Cornucopia, 7", small silver paper label...$75.00–100.00
Vase, 7", small silver paper label...$75.00–100.00
Vase, 8", silver paper label $150.00–175.00
Vase, 7½", no mark $100.00–125.00
Vase, 5½", no mark...$80.00–100.00

ROW 4:

Vase, 8", silver paper label $100.00–125.00
Vase, 8", no mark $150.00–175.00
Vase, 10", no mark $250.00–275.00
Vase, 8", no mark $150.00–175.00
Vase, 8", no mark $150.00–175.00

LAUREL, 1934

Vase, 10", small silver paper label
$350.00–400.00
Vase, 9½", small silver paper label
$275.00–300.00
Vase, 6½", no mark
$200.00–225.00
Bowl, 3½", no mark
$200.00–225.00

TOURMALINE, 1933

MONTACELLO*, 1931

Basket, 6½", no mark
blue, *$400.00–450.00*
brown, *$450.00–500.00*
Vase, 5", no mark
$250.00–300.00
Vase, 8½", no mark
$350.00–400.00
Vase, 10½", black paper label
$450.00–500.00
*Company spelling

Left:
Vase, 14½", no mark
$400.00–450.00
Bowl, 11" x 3", no mark
$175.00–200.00

Below:
Vase, 8", no mark
$200.00–225.00
Vase, 12½", no mark
$350.00–400.00
Vase, 9½", no mark
$250.00–300.00

VELMOSS, 1935

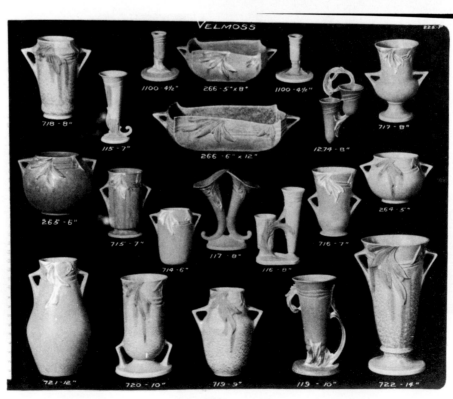

SUNFLOWER, 1930

ROW 1:
Vase, 4", no mark $225.00–275.00
Vase, 5", no mark $225.00–275.00
Vase, 5", no mark $225.00–275.00
Bowl, 4", no mark $250.00–300.00

ROW 2:
Candlesticks, 4", no mark ....$400.00–450.00 pair
Console, 3" x 12½", small black paper label $275.00–325.00

ROW 3:
Vase, 5", no mark $325.00–375.00
Window Box, 3½" x 11", no mark $350.00–450.00
Vase, 6", no mark $275.00–325.00

ROW 4:
Vase, 7", no mark $400.00–500.00
Vase, 10", no mark $550.00–650.00
Vase, 6", no mark $350.00–450.00

ROW 1:   **PINECONE, 1931**

Planter, 5", Roseville impressed, #124 ....*$200.00–225.00*
Centerpiece/candleholder, 6", Roseville impressed, #324 ....*$650.00–750.00*
Bowl, 4½", Roseville impressed, #320–5 ....*$175.00–200.00*
ROW 2:
Bowl, 4½", Roseville in relief, #457–7 ....*$175.00–200.00*
Window Box, 3½" x 15½", Roseville in relief, #431–15..*$350.00–400.00*
Ashtray, 4½", Roseville in relief, #499 ....*$100.00–125.00*
ROW 3:
Candlestick, 2½", Roseville impressed, #112–3..*$125.00–150.00*
Mug, 4", Roseville in relief, #960–4 ....*$150.00–200.00*
Pitcher, 9½", Roseville impressed, #708–9 ....*$700.00–800.00*
Tumbler, 5", Roseville in relief, #414 ....*$150.00–200.00*
Candlestick, 5", Roseville impressed, #1099–4½..*$100.00–150.00*
ROW 4:
Vase, 10½", Roseville impressed, #747–10..*$350.00–400.00*
Vase, 14½", Roseville impressed, #850–14..*$500.00–600.00*
Pitcher, 10½", Roseville in relief, #485–10 ....*$325.00–375.00*

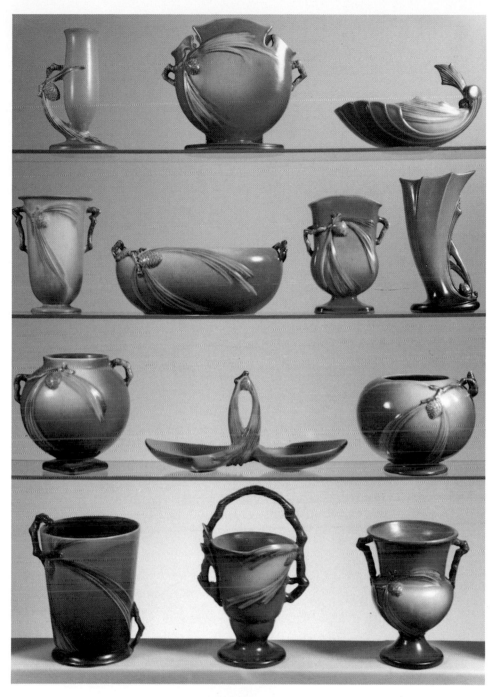

PINECONE, 1931

ROW 1:
Bud Vase, 7½", Roseville in relief, #479–7, in Apple Blossom pink, the only true pink Pine Cone reported....$300.00–400.00
Pillow Vase, 8", Roseville impressed, #845–8 ....$300.00–350.00
Boat Dish, 9", Roseville in relief, #427–8 ....$200.00–250.00

ROW 2:
Vase, 7", Roseville impressed, #907–7 ....$150.00–175.00
Console, 11", silver paper label $300.00–350.00
Vase, 7", Roseville impressed, #121–7 ....$225.00–250.00
Vase, 8½", Roseville in relief, #490–8...$200.00–225.00

ROW 3:
Vase, 7", Roseville impressed, #745–7 ....$350.00–400.00
Double Tray, 13", no mark $225.00–275.00
Vase, 5", no mark..$200.00–250.00

ROW 4:
Vase, 8", silver paper label..$225.00–250.00
Basket, 11", Roseville impressed, #353–11...$375.00–425.00
Vase, 8", Roseville impressed, #908–8 ....$250.00–275.00

TOPEO, 1934

ROW 1:   *Opposite page*
Bowl, 3" x 11½", no mark...$115.00–140.00

ROW 2:
Vase, 7", silver paper label $150.00–200.00
Bowl, 4" x 13", silver paper label $175.00–250.00
Vase, 6", silver paper label $165.00–200.00

ROW 3:
Vase, 14", no mark $450.00–550.00
Vase, 9", no mark $175.00–225.00
Vase, 15", no mark $500.00–600.00

Center right:
Vase, 9", Trial color indicated by series of numbers in red crayon.......................................$300.00–400.00

Below:
Console, 13", no mark $200.00–250.00
Double Candlestick, 5", small silver paper label...$100.00–125.00

It has always been a question in the minds of Roseville collectors — were those Topeo shapes glazed in red truly Topeo or were they actually from a separate line? We still don't have the answer to that question, but two new discoveries seem to add credence to the theory that a red glazed line did exist. The label photographed below revealed the name of the elegant Art-Deco "Artcraft" line. You will see other examples of this line in the color plates — in a warm mottled tan and a beautiful blue green similar to the Earlam glaze. The red piece on the opposite page is as incongruous with these soft glazes as Red Topeo seems to that line. But until an answer is found, Red Topeo…Red Artcraft, seem to be the most logical terms of reference.

TOPEO, 1934

ARTCRAFT

Left:
Jardiniere, 4", silver paper label
$150.00–175.00

LUFFA, 1934

MOSS, 1930s

Urn, 6", Roseville impressed, #290–6 ....$200.00–225.00
Pillow Vase, 8", Roseville impressed, #781–8 ....$200.00–225.00
Candlestick, 2", Roseville impressed, #1104...$75.00–85.00
Triple Bud Vase, 7", Roseville impressed, #1108 ....$350.00–400.00

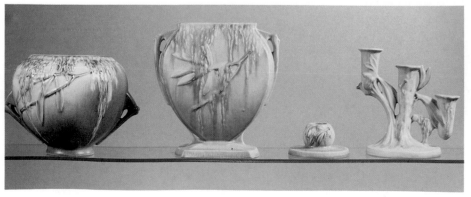

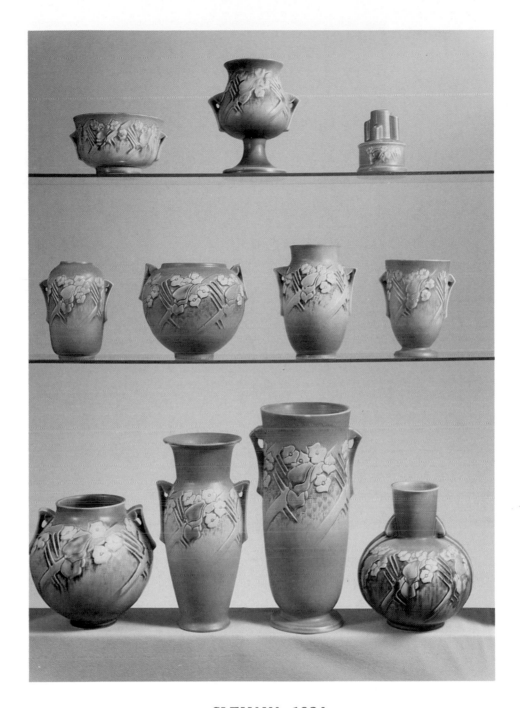

CLEMANA, 1934

ROW 1:

Bowl, 4½" x 6½", Roseville impressed, #281–5 ....$200.00–225.00
Vase, 7½", Roseville impressed, #112–7 ....$275.00–300.00
Flower Frog, 4", Roseville impressed, #23 ....$150.00–175.00

ROW 2:

Vase, 6½", Roseville impressed, #749–6...$200.00–225.00
Vase, 6½", Roseville impressed, #280–6...$250.00–300.00
Vase, 7½", Roseville impressed, #752–7...$250.00–300.00
Vase, 6½", Roseville impressed, #750–6...$200.00–250.00

ROW 3:

Vase, 8½", Roseville impressed, #754–8..$300.00–350.00
Vase, 12½", Roseville impressed, #758–12..$450.00–500.00
Vase, 14, Roseville impressed, #759–14 ....$600.00–700.00
Vase, 9½", Roseville impressed, #756–9..$300.00–350.00

ORIAN, 1935

ROW 1:
Vase, 6", Roseville impressed, #733–6
$100.00–125.00
Vase, 9", small silver label
$140.00–165.00
Candleholder, 4½", no mark
$85.00–95.00

ROW 2:
Vase, 7", small silver paper label
$100.00–125.00
Console Bowl, 5", no mark
$175.00–200.00
Vase, 6½", Roseville impressed, #733–6
$100.00–125.00

Opposite page, top

Vase, 12½", no mark $200.00–250.00
Vase, 10½", no mark $150.00–200.00
Vase, 7½", no mark $150.00–175.00
Comport, 4½" x 10½", Roseville impressed, #272–10 ....$100.00–125.00

FALLINE, 1933

ROW 1:   *Opposite page, center*
Vase, 6", small silver label..$375.00–425.00
Vase, 6", no mark $325.00–375.00
Candleholder, 4", no mark $150.00–200.00
Bowl, 11", no mark $225.00–250.00

ROW 2:
Vase, 8", small silver label...$375.00–425.00
Vase, 12½", small silver label $800.00–900.00
Vase, 9", no mark $500.00–600.00
Vase, 7½", small silver label $375.00–425.00

FERELLA, 1931

ROW 1:   *Opposite page, bottom*
Vase, 6", no mark $300.00–350.00
Lamp base, 10½", no mark, blended blue and green glaze is not a standard Ferella color $900.00–800.00
Vase, 8", no mark $450.00–500.00

ROW 2:
Vase, 6", small black paper label...$250.00–275.00
Candlesticks, 4½", no mark ....$450.00–500.00 pair
Bowl/Frog, 5", no mark $350.00–400.00
Vase, 4", no mark $200.00–225.00

ORIAN, 1935

FALLINE, 1933

FERELLA, 1931

117

THORN APPLE, 1930s

ROW 1:
Vase, 8½", Roseville impressed, #816–8
$150.00–225.00
Double Bud Vase, 5½", Roseville
impressed, #1119, *$100.00–125.00*
Hanging Basket, 7" wide
$350.00–400.00
Triple Bud Vase, 6" Roseville impressed,
#1120, *$150.00–200.00*

ROW 2:
Bowl Vase, 6½", Roseville impressed,
#305–6, *$125.00–175.00*
Vase, 10½", Roseville impressed,
#822–10, *$250.00–300.00*
Vase, 9½", Roseville impressed, #820–9
$175.00–225.00

EARLAM, 1930

ROW 1:
Vase, 4", no mark
$95.00–110.00
Vase, 6", no mark
$150.00–175.00
Candlestick, 4", black paper label
$225.00–275.00

ROW 2:
Bowl, 3" x 11½", no mark
$135.00–160.00
Vase, 9", no mark
$325.00–375.00
Planter, 5½" x 10½", no mark
$125.00–150.00

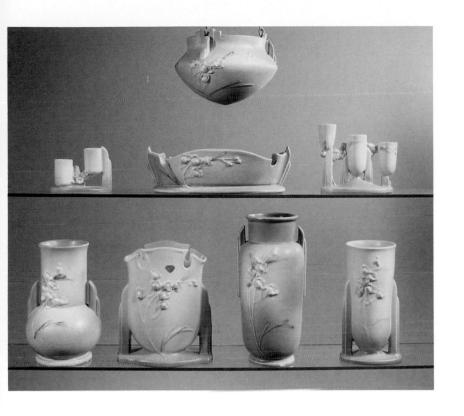

IXIA, 1930s

ROW 1:
Hanging Basket, 7"
$175.00–225.00
Double Candlestick, 3", Roseville impressed,
#1127, *$85.00–95.00*
Console Bowl, 3½" x 10½", Roseville
impressed, #330–7, *$100.00–125.00* ·
Candleholder/Bud Vase, 5", Roseville
impressed, #1128, *$125.00–150.00*

ROW 2:
Vase, 8½", Roseville impressed, #857–8
$125.00–150.00
Vase, 8½", same mark, #858–8, silver paper
label, *$125.00–150.00*
Vase, 10½", Roseville impressed, #862–10
$150.00–175.00
Vase, 8½", Roseville impressed, #856–8
$125.00–150.00

WINDSOR, 1931

ROW 1:
Bowl, 3½" x 10½", no mark
$150.00–175.00
Basket, 4½", small black paper label
$300.00–350.00
Bowl, 3" x 10", small silver paper label
$150.00–175.00

ROW 2:
Vase, 6", no mark
$200.00–250.00
Vase, 7", small black paper label
$500.00–600.00
Lamp base 7", no mark
$500.00–600.00

MODERNE, 1930s

ROW 1:
Triple Candleholder, 6", Roseville
impressed, #1112, *$200.00–225.00*
Vase, 6½, Roseville impressed, #299
$125.00–175.00
Vase, 6½", Roseville impressed, #787
$100.00–120.00

ROW 2:
Comport, 6", Roseville impressed, #297–6
$100.00–150.00
Vase, 8½", same mark #796–8, small silver
paper label, *$125.00–150.00*
Vase, 6", Roseville impressed, #789–6
$100.00–125.00
Comport, 5", Roseville impressed, #295
$100.00–125.00

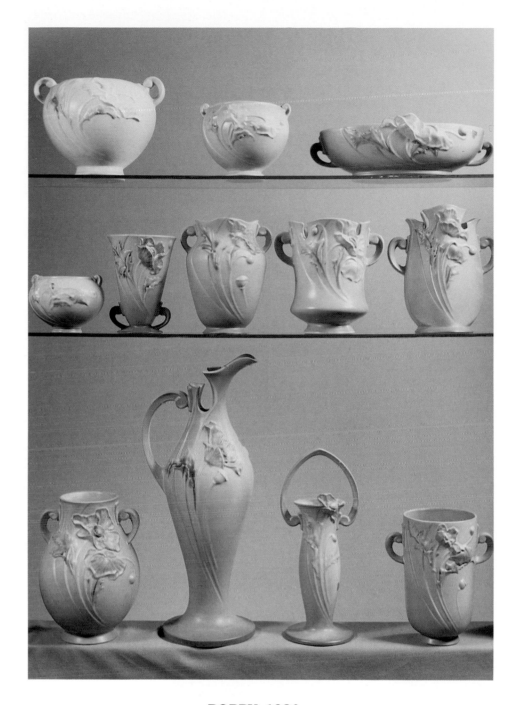

POPPY, 1930

ROW 1:
Vase, 6½", Roseville impressed, #335–6..$100.00–125.00
Vase, 5", Roseville impressed, #642–4..$85.00–95.00
Bowl, 12", Roseville impressed, #336–10..$150.00–175.00

ROW 2:
Bowl, 3½", Roseville impressed, #642–3 ....$75.00–85.00
Vase, 6", Roseville impressed, #346–6..$125.00–150.00
Vase, 7½", Roseville impressed, #368–7..$150.00–175.00
Vase, 7½", Roseville impressed, #869–7..$150.00–175.00
Vase, 8", Roseville impressed, #870–8..$175.00–200.00

ROW 3:
Vase, 9", Roseville impressed, #872–9..$225.00–250.00
Ewer, 18½", Roseville impressed, #880–18..$650.00–750.00
Basket, 12½", Roseville impressed, #348–12..$350.00–400.00
Vase, 8", Roseville impressed, #871–8..$175.00–200.00

Right:
Vase, 6½, Roseville impressed, #761–6
$100.00–150.00
Vase, 7", Roseville impressed, #760–6
$100.00–150.00

PRIMROSE, 1932

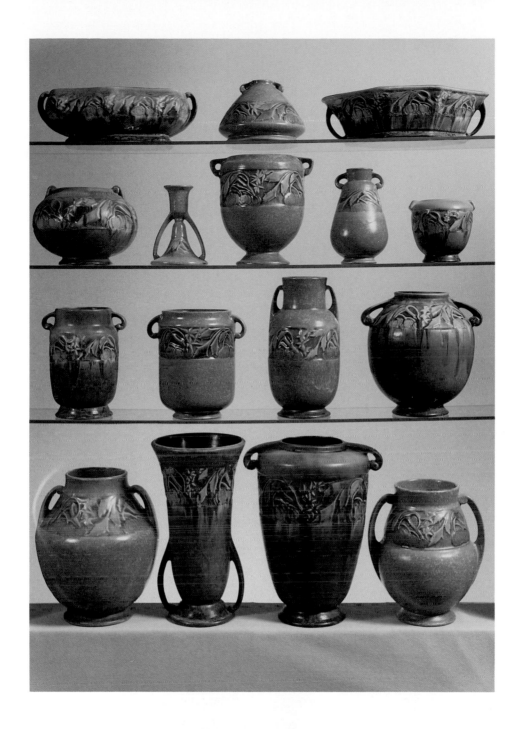

BANEDA, 1933

ROW 1:
Bowl, 3½" x 10", no mark $350.00–400.00
Vase, 4½", silver paper label $275.00–325.00
Bowl, 3" x 11", no mark $375.00–425.00

ROW 2:
Vase, 5", silver paper label $350.00–400.00
Candleholder, 5½", silver paper label..........$250.00–275.00
Vase, 7", no mark $475.00–525.00
Vase, 6", no mark $300.00–350.00
Vase, 4", no mark $250.00–275.00

ROW 3:
Vase, 7", no mark $400.00–450.00
Vase, 7", silver paper label $425.00–475.00
Vase, 9", silver paper label $475.00–525.00
Vase, 8", no mark $500.00–600.00

ROW 4:
Vase, 10", small silver paper label.................$600.00–650.00
Vase, 12", small silver paper label.................$750.00–850.00
Vase, 12", no mark $1,000.00–1,250.00
Vase, 9", small silver paper label...................$500.00–550.00

TEASEL, 1936

Vase, 12", Roseville impressed, #888–12
$250.00–275.00
Vase, 10", Roseville impressed, #887–10
$175.00–225.00
Vase, 6", Roseville impressed, #881–6
$90.00–110.00

BLACKBERRY, 1933

ROW 1:
Vase, 6", small silver paper label
$300.00–350.00
Hanging Basket, 4½" x 6½"
$750.00–850.00
Basket
$700.00–800.00

ROW 2:
Jardiniere, 7", no mark
$325.00–375.00
Jardiniere, 6", no mark
$300.00–350.00
Jardiniere, 4", small silver paper label
$200.00–250.00

MORNING GLORY, 1935

ROW 1:
Candlestick, 5", no mark
$150.00–200.00
Console Bowl, 4½" x 11½", no mark
$300.00–350.00
Pot, 5", no mark
$200.00–250.00

ROW 2:
Basket, 10½", small silver paper label
$400.00–500.00
Vase, 15", no mark
$850.00–950.00
Pillow Vase, 7", small silver paper label
$225.00–275.00

DAWN, 1937

Right:
Ewer, 16", Roseville impressed, #834–16
$450.00–550.00

Below:
Vase, 12", Roseville impressed, #833–12
$150.00–200.00
Bowl, 16", Roseville impressed, #318–14
$125.00–175.00

IVORY II, 1937

Right:
Hanging Basket, 7"
$75.00–100.00
Dog, 6½", no mark
$300.00–400.00
Nude, 9", no mark
$400.00–500.00

Below:
ROW 1:
Cornucopia, 5½" x 12", Roseville in relief, #2
$45.00–60.00
Jardiniere, 4", Roseville in relief, #574–4
$40.00–50.00
Vase, 6½", Roseville impressed, #271–6
$55.00–75.00

ROW 2:
Vase, 7", no mark
$50.00–75.00
Candlestick, 5½", Roseville impressed, #1122–5
$30.00–40.00
Ewer, 10½", Roseville impressed, #941–10
$50.00–75.00
Candlestick, 2½", Roseville impressed
$25.00–35.00
Jardiniere, 6", no mark
$45.00–50.00

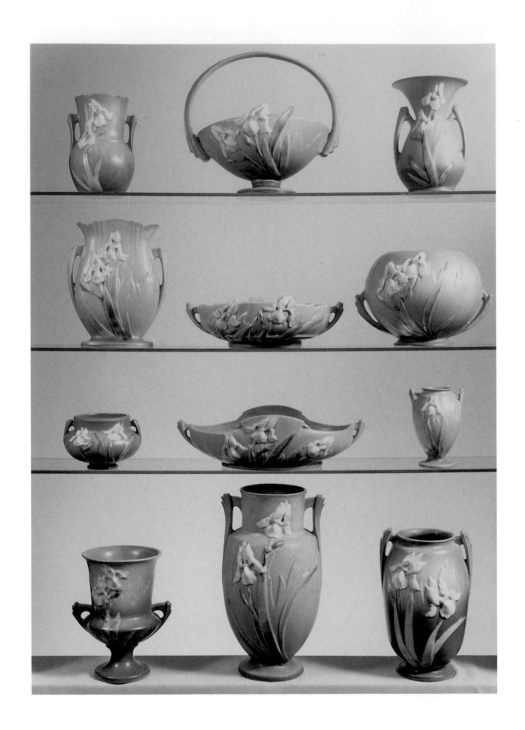

IRIS, 1938

ROW 1:
Vase, 6½", Roseville impressed, #917–6..........*$100.00–125.00*
Basket, 9½", Roseville impressed, #355–10 ....*$250.00–300.00*
Vase, 7½", Roseville impressed, #920–7..........*$125.00–175.00*

ROW 2:
Pillow Vase, 8½", Roseville impressed, #922–8 ..*$150.00–200.00*
Console Bowl, 3" x 10", Roseville in relief,
   #361–8 ....*$100.00–125.00*
Vase, 6½", Roseville impressed, #358–6..........*$150.00–200.00*

ROW 3:
Bowl Vase, 3½", Roseville in relief, #647–3.........*$75.00–85.00*
Console Bowl, 3½" x 12½", Roseville impressed,
   #362–10 ....*125.00–175.00*
Vase, 5", Roseville impressed, #915–5 ....*$75.00–85.00*

ROW 4:
Vase, 8", Roseville impressed, #923–8 ....*$150.00–175.00*
Vase, 12½", Roseville impressed, #928–12......*$225.00–325.00*
Vase, 10", Roseville impressed, #924–9 ....*$175.00–250.00*

BLEEDING HEART, 1938

Woman's Home Companion July 1940

ROW 1:
Hanging Basket, 8" wide...$250.00–300.00
Bowl Vase, 3½", #651–3...$85.00–95.00
Vase, 8", #969–8...$150.00–175.00
Bowl Vase, 4", #377–4...$90.00–110.00
Vase, 8½", #968–9...$175.00–200.00
Vase, 6½", #964–6...$150.00–175.00

ROW 2:
Candlestick, 5", #1139–4½, silver paper label.................................$150.00–175.00 *pair*
Console Bowl/Frog, 17", #384–14; Frog, #40 ....$200.00–250.00

ROW 3:
Basket, 9½", #360–10 ....$225.00–275.00
Vase, 15", #976–15 ....$350.00–400.00
Plate, 10½", #381–10...$150.00–175.00

Mark: Roseville in relief

COLUMBINE, 1940

ROW 1:   Vase, 7½", #17–7 . . . . $125.00–150.00
Hanging Basket, 8½". $200.00–250.00
Vase, 8", #151–8 . . . . $175.00–200.00

ROW 2:   Bookend Planter, 5", #8 . . . . $125.00–175.00
Candleholders, 5", #1146–4½ $125.00–150.00
Cornucopia, 5½", #149–6 . . . . $85.00–95.00
Mark: Roseville in relief

FUCHSIA, 1939

ROW 1:
Vase, 6", Roseville impressed, #893–6 ....$125.00–150.00
Vase, 6", Roseville in relief, #891–6 ....$125.00–150.00
Vase, 6", Roseville in relief, #892–6 ....$125.00–150.00

ROW 2:
Candlesticks, 2", Roseville impressed, #1132, pair ....$125.00–150.00 pair
Console Bowl, 3½" x 12½", Roseville impressed, #351–10 ....$175.00–200.00

ROW 3:
Candlesticks, 5½", Roseville impressed, #1133–5, pair ....$200.00–250.00 pair
Console Bowl/Frog, 4" x 15½", Roseville in relief, #353–14; Frog, #37 ....$275.00–325.00

ROW 4:
Vase, 8", Roseville impressed, #879–8 ....$250.00–275.00
Vase, 8½", Roseville impressed, #896–8 ....$200.00–250.00
Vase, 8" Roseville impressed, #898–8 ....$250.00–275.00

COSMOS, 1940

ROW 1:

Hanging Basket, 7" $200.00–250.00
Vase, 8", Roseville impressed, #905–8..$125.00–150.00
Vase, 5", Roseville in relief, #945–5...$100.00–125.00
Vase, 4", Roseville in relief, #375–4...$150.00–175.00
Vase, 6½", no mark...$150.00–175.00
Vase, 12½", Roseville in relief, #956–12 ....$450.00–550.00

ROW 2:

Vase, 4", Roseville in relief, #134–4...$95.00–110.00
Console Bowl, 15½", Roseville impressed, #374–14 ....$200.00–250.00
Flower Frog, 3½", no mark $100.00–125.00

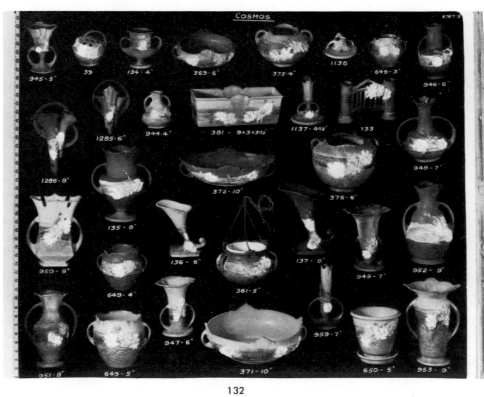

WHITE ROSE, 1940

BETTER HOMES & GARDENS, OCTOBER, 1940

ROW 1:
Vase, 4", #978–4 ....$80.00–90.00
Vase, 5", #980–6 ....$90.00–110.00
Basket, 7½", #362–8 ....$200.00–250.00
Vase, 6", #979–6 ....$110.00–135.00
Candlestick, 4½", #1142–4½..$65.00–75.00

ROW 2:
Vase, 7", #388–7 ....$150.00–200.00
Vase, 8", #984–8 ....$150.00–200.00
Vase, 8½", #985–8 ....$150.00–200.00

ROW 3:
Double Bud Vase, 4½", #148 ..$85.00–95.00
Console, Frog, 16½", #393–12,
    Frog, #41 ....$150.00–200.00
Double Candleholder, 4",
    #1143 ....$125.00–150.00

ROW 4:
Vase 12½", #991–12............$250.00–300.00
Vase, 15½", #992–15..........$300.00–400.00
Vase, 9", #987–9 ....$150.00–200.00

Mark: Roseville in relief

Company placard

ROW 1:
Basket, 8½", #807–8
$125.00–150.00
Vase, 6", #881–6
$75.00–85.00
Bowl Vase, 7", #842–7
$125.00–150.00

ROW 2:
Planter, 10½", #828–10
$95.00–120.00
Planter, 11½", #827–8
$95.00–120.00
Cornucopia, 4½", #857–4
$85.00–95.00

ROW 3:
Candlestick, 3", #851–3
$50.00–60.00
Console Bowl, 12½", #829–12
$115.00–140.00
Candlestick, 3", #851–3
$50.00–60.00
Double Vase, 4", #858
$95.00–115.00

ROW 4:
Vase, 7", #874–7
$100.00–125.00
Vase, 10", #885–10
$125.00–150.00
Vase, 15½", #888–16
$250.00–350.00
Vase, 8", #884–8
$125.00–150.00
Mark: Roseville in relief

FOXGLOVE, 1942

ROW 1:

Tray, 8½", Roseville impressed $95.00–110.00
Hanging Basket, 6½" $250.00–300.00
Cornucopia, 6", Roseville in relief, #166–6 ....$125.00–150.00

ROW 2:

Tray, 15" wide, Roseville impressed...$135.00–160.00
Flower Frog, 4", Roseville in relief, #46 ....$110.00–135.00
Tray, 11", Roseville impressed $110.00–135.00

ROW 3:

Vase, 12½", Roseville in relief, #52–12 ....$300.00–350.00
Vase, 14", Roseville in relief, #58–14...$400.00–450.00
Vase, 10", Roseville in relief, #51–10..$175.00–225.00
Vase, 8½", Roseville in relief, #47–8 ....$125.00–175.00

PEONY, 1942

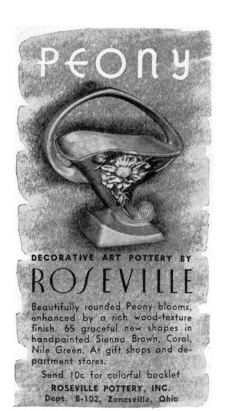

BETTER HOMES & GARDENS, OCTOBER, 1942

ROW 1:   *Mark: Roseville in relief*
Bookend, 5½", #11, each $95.00–110.00
Conch Shell, 9½", #436 ....$110.00–135.00
Tray, 8" $75.00–100.00

ROW 2:
Planter, 10", #387–8 ....$85.00–95.00
Bowl, 11", #430–10 ....$100.00–125.00

ROW 3:
Double Candleholder, 5", #115–3 ....$125.00–150.00
Mug, 3½", #2–3½ $100.00–125.00
Pitcher, 7½", #1326–7½ $275.00–325.00
Frog, 4", #47 ....$85.00–95.00

ROW 4:
Vase, 8", #169–8 ....$125.00–150.00
Basket, 11", #379–12 ....$250.00–275.00
Vase, 14", #68–14 ....$250.00–300.00

MAGNOLIA, 1943

ROW 1:
Planter, 8½", #388–6 . . . . *$85.00–95.00*
Planter, 6", #183–6 . . . . *$90.00–110.00*
Candlestick, 5", #1157–4½ . . . *$75.00–85.00*
Candlestick, 2½", #1156–2½". *$50.00–60.00*

ROW 2:
Ashtray, 7", #28 . . . . *$100.00–125.00*
Console Bowl, 14½", #5–10 . *$125.00–175.00*
Cornucopia, 6", #184–6 . . . . . . *$85.00–95.00*

ROW 3:
Vase, 6", #180–6 . . . . *$95.00–110.00*
Flower Frog, 5½", #182–5 . . *$95.00–110.00*
Conch Shell, 6½", #453–6 . . *$95.00–110.00*
Vase, 6", #88–6 . . . . *$95.00–110.00*

ROW 4:
Basket, 12", #386–12 . . . . . . *$200.00–225.00*
Ewer, 10", #14–10 . . . . *$175.00–200.00*
Vase, 8", #91–8 . . . . *$125.00–150.00*

Mark: Roseville in relief

WATER LILY, 1943

Vase, 9", #78–9 ....$200.00–225.00
Candlesticks, 5", #1155–4½ ....$150.00–175.00 pair
Hanging Basket, 9", U.S.A. $175.00–225.00
Frog, 4½", #48 ....$85.00–95.00

Mark: Roseville in relief

WATER LILY

Beautiful new decorative art pottery that will distinguish your loveliest setting. Fifty graceful shapes —choice of exquisite, hand-painted colors — Rose, Ciel Blue or Walnut Brown. Modestly priced at department stores and gift shops.

Send 10c for pottery booklet
ROSEVILLE POTTERY, INC.
Dept. B-43, Zanesville, Ohio

ROSEVILLE
DECORATIVE ART POTTERY

BETTER HOMES & GARDENS, APRIL, 1943

FREESIA, 1945

ROW 1:
Flower Pot/Saucer, 5½",
  #670–5 ....$125.00–150.00
Basket, 7", #390–7............$125.00–150.00
Bowl, 4", #669–4 ....$85.00–95.00

ROW 2:
Bowl, 8½", #464–6 ....$75.00–85.00
Bowl, 11", #465–8 ....$110.00–135.00

ROW 3:
Candlesticks, 2", #1160–2..$95.00–110.00 pair
Console, 16½", #469–14 ..$150.00–175.00

ROW 4:
Vase, 5", #463–5 ....$110.00–125.00
Vase, 7", #119–7 ....$95.00–115.00
Window Box, 10½",
  #1392–8 ....$85.00–95.00

ROW 5:
Vase, 8", #121–8 ....$110.00–135.00
Vase, 9½", #123–9 ....$125.00–150.00
Vase, 10½", #125–10 ....$150.00–175.00
Vase, 9", #124–9 ....$125.00–150.00

Mark: Roseville in relief

ROZANE PATTERN, 1940s

Vase, 12", Roseville in relief, #10–12 ....$100.00–125.00
Bowl, 7½", Roseville in relief, #8–8; shown with ornament, 5", Roseville in relief, #1 ....$150.00–175.00
Vase, 8½", Roseville in relief, #5–8 ....$85.00–95.00

Company booklet featuring Zephyr Lily ewer

ZEPHYR LILY, 1946

ROW 1:
Fan Vase, 6½", #205–6...................................$90.00–115.00
Hanging Basket, 7½"....................................$150.00–175.00
Pillow Vase, 7", #206–7.................................$100.00–125.00

ROW 2:
Candlesticks, 2", #1162–2......................$95.00–110.00 pair
Console Bowl, 16½", #479–14.....................$175.00–200.00
Bud Vase, 7½", #201–7...................................$75.00–85.00

ROW 3:
Vase, 8½", #133–8...$75.00–100.00
Tray, 14½", impressed Roseville..................$125.00–150.00
Cornucopia, 8½", #204–8................................$85.00–95.00

ROW 4:
Vase, 9½", #135–9...$100.00–125.00
Vase, 12", #139–12.......................................$150.00–175.00
Vase, 12½", #140–12....................................$175.00–200.00
Vase, 8½", #202–8...$125.00–150.00

Mark: Roseville in relief

CLEMATIS, 1944

The American Home, Feb. '45

ROW 1:

Console Bowl, 14", #458–10	$100.00–125.00
Candleholder, 2½", #1155–2	$50.00–60.00
Console Bowl, 9", #456–6	$65.00–75.00

ROW 2:

Flower Arranger, 5½", #102–5	$65.00–75.00
Flower Pot, 5½", #668–5	$110.00–135.00
Vase, 6", #103–6	$65.00–75.00
Flower Frog, 4½", #50	$65.00–75.00
Vase, 6½", #102–6	$75.00–85.00

Mark: Roseville in relief

Company brochure and envelope

SNOWBERRY, 1946

ROW 1:
Vase, 6", #IRB–6 ....$100.00–125.00
Pillow Vase, 6½", #1FH–6....................$95.00–110.00
Flowerpot, 5½", #1PS–5 ....$125.00–150.00

ROW 2:
Candlesticks, 4½", #1CS–2 ....$125.00–150.00 pair
Console Bowl, 11", #1BL–8 ....$90.00–110.00

Mark: Roseville in relief

ROW 3:
Vase, 6", #V–6 ....$85.00–95.00
Tray, 14", #1BL–12 ....$125.00–150.00
Vase, 7½", #1V2–7..............................$95.00–110.00

ROW 4:
Vase, 12½", #1V1–12 ....$175.00–200.00
Ewer, 16", #1TK–15 ....$375.00–400.00
Basket, 12½", #1BK–12 ....$175.00–225.00
Vase, 8½", #1UR–8..............................$140.00–165.00

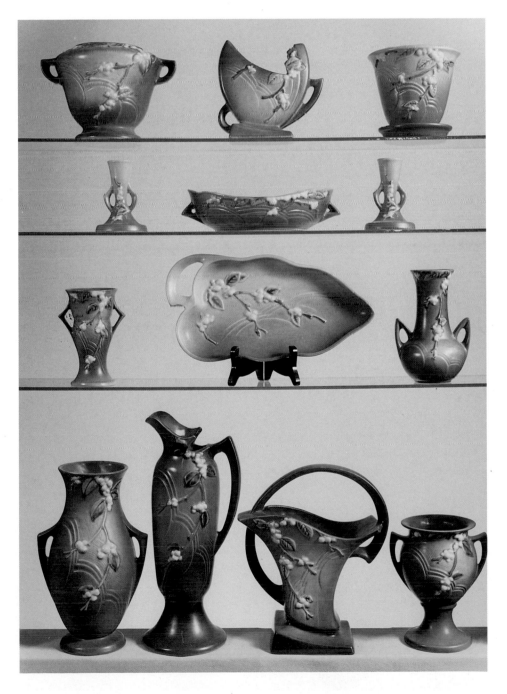

new . . and beautiful!

Snowberry

So exquisitely different . . . so tastefully decorative! Round white berries on a dainty twig. 52 lovely pieces—hand-painted under glaze— in Persian Blue, Fern Green, Dusty Rose. The right gift choice for every occasion! At better stores.

APPLE BLOSSOM, 1948

ROW 1:
Bowl, 2½" x 6½", #326–6 ....$85.00–95.00
Jardiniere, 6", #342–6 ....$115.00–140.00
Window Box, 2½" x 10½", #368–8 ....$85.00–95.00

ROW 2:
Vase, 10", #388–10 ....$150.00–175.00
Vase, 15½", #392–15 ....$375.00–425.00
Vase, 12½", #390–12 ....$200.00–250.00

Mark: Roseville in relief

GARDENIA, late 1940s

ROW 1: Hanging Basket, 6" $200.00–225.00
Bowl, 5", #641–5 ....$90.00–110.00
Window Box, 3" x 8½", #658–8 ....$85.00–95.00
Vase, 8", #683–8 ....$115.00–140.00

ROW 2: Vase, 10", #658–10 ....$125.00–150.00
Tray, 15", #631–14 ....$140.00–165.00
Vase, 10½", #686–10 ....$150.00–175.00

ROW 3: Basket, 12", #610–12 ....$200.00–225.00
Vase, 12", #687–12 ....$150.00–175.00
Vase, 14½", #689–14 ....$250.00–300.00

Mark: Roseville in relief

FLOWERPOT

Jardiniere, 7½", #90–4
$40.00–45.00
Pitcher, 5", #1101–5
$40.00–45.00
Pitcher, 5", #1102–5
$50.00–60.00
Cornucopia, 3" x 6½", #1013–6
$40.00–45.00

MAYFAIR, late 1940s

ROW 1:
Jardiniere, 4", #1109–4
$35.00–40.00
Planter, 3½" x 8½", #1113–8
$50.00–60.00

ROW 2:
Flower Pot, 4½", #71–4
$40.00–45.00
Vase, 7", #1104–9
$95.00–110.00
Teapot, 5", #1121
$95.00–110.00

ROW 3:
Candlestick, 4½", #115–1
$15.00–20.00
Bowl, 7", impressed mark
$25.00–30.00
Bowl, 10", impressed, #1119–9
$50.00–60.00
Vase, 12½", #1106–12
$65.00–75.00

Mark: Roseville in relief

BUSHBERRY, 1948

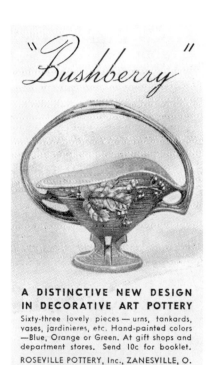

ROW 1:
Double Cornucopia, 6", #155–8 ....$125.00–150.00
Candlestick, 2", #144–7–CS............................$60.00–70.00
Hanging Basket, 7", U.S.A. $325.00–375.00
Vase, 4", no mark $65.00–75.00
Vase, 7", #32–7 ....$100.00–125.00

ROW 2:
Double Bud Vase, 4½", #158–4½ $100.00–125.00
Console Bowl, 13", #385–10 ....$125.00–175.00
Planter, 6½", #383–6 ....$90.00–110.00

ROW 3:
Cider Pitcher, 8½", #1325 ....$300.00–350.00
Mug, 3½", #1–3½ $100.00–125.00

ROW 3: *(continued)*
Vase, 6", #156–6 ....$125.00–150.00
Bud Vase, 7½", #152–7 ....$100.00–125.00
Bowl Vase, 6", #411–6 ....$125.00–150.00

ROW 4:
Vase, 8", #34–8 ....$125.00–150.00
Vase, 12½", #38–12 ....$250.00–300.00
Vase, 14½", #39–14 ....$400.00–450.00
Vase, 8", #157–8 ....$125.00–150.00

Mark: Roseville in relief

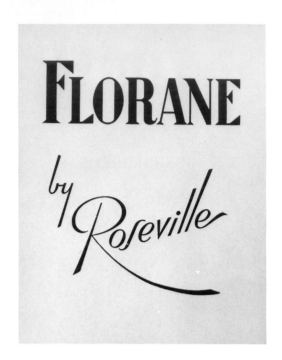

FLORANE, late line (1949?)

The only item on either of these catalogue pages that is at all reminiscent of the old Florane is Bud Base, #79. And the only clue as to its time of production is perhaps #649 in the lower left hand corner. We have found it a not uncommon practice by other potteries to use a dating code of this type. The colors are very soft shades of tan, blue, and green, with a slightly deeper tan lining for contrast.

Left		*Right*	
ROW 1:		**ROW 1:**	
Bowl, 10"	$30.00–35.00	Planter Box, 6"	$25.00–30.00
Bowl, 9"	$50.00–60.00	Bowl, 7"	$20.00–25.00
ROW 2:		Planter, 6"	$25.00–30.00
Bowl, 6"	$20.00–25.00	**ROW 2:**	
Bowl, 12"	$65.00–75.00	Planter, 10"	$45.00–50.00
Bowl, 8"	$20.00–25.00	Planter, 4"	$20.00–25.00
ROW 3:		Planter, 8"	$35.00–40.00
Vase, 6"	$30.00–35.00	**ROW 3:**	
Bud Vase, 7"	$30.00–35.00	Pot, 4"	$20.00–25.00
Vase, 7"	$40.00–45.00	Pot, 5"	$25.00–30.00
ROW 4:		Pot, 6"	$35.00–40.00
Vase, 9"	$75.00–90.00	Bowl, 10"	$25.00–30.00
Vase, 11"	$75.00–100.00	**ROW 4:**	
Vase, 14"	$90.00–115.00	Sand Jar, 12"	$100.00–135.00
		Jar, 10"	$100.00–125.00
		Jar, 8"	$90.00–115.00

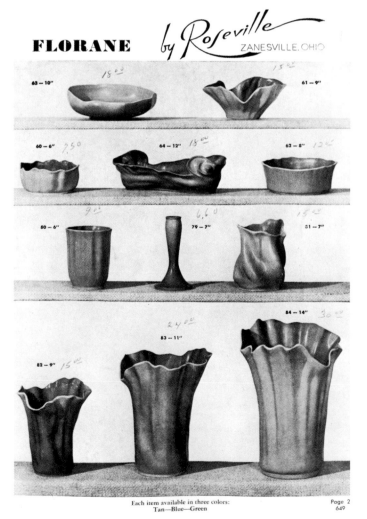

Each item available in three colors:
Tan—Blue—Green

Page 2
649

Each item available in three colors:
Tan—Blue—Green

Page 1
649

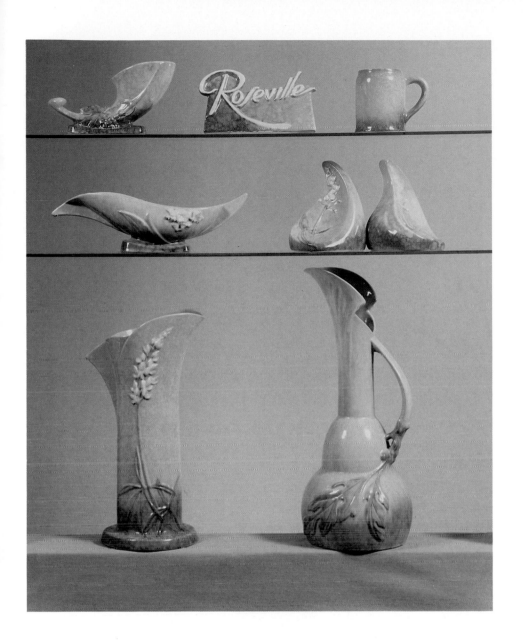

WINCRAFT, 1948

ROW 1:

Cornucopia, 9" x 5", #221–8................................$85.00–95.00
Dealer Sign, 4½" x 8", no mark $1,500.00–1,750.00
Mug, 4½", no mark $50.00–60.00

ROW 2:

Bowl, 4" x 13½", #227–10 ....$90.00–110.00
Bookends, 6½", #259.......................................$150.00–175.00

ROW 3:

Vase, 16", #288–15...$250.00–275.00
Ewer, 19", #218–18...$500.00–600.00

Right:

Vase, 7", #274–7...$150.00–175.00
Basket, 12", #210–12 ....$250.00–300.00

Mark: Roseville in relief

Company placard

ARTWOOD, late 1940s (?)

ROW 1:
3-pc. Planter Set; side section, 4", #1050; Center section, 6",
#1051–6, *$110.00–125.00*
Planter, 6½" x 8½", #1054–8½
$85.00–95.00

ROW 2:
Planter, 7" x 9½", #1055–9
$85.00–95.00
Vase, 8", #1057–8
$85.00–95.00
Planter, 6½" x 10½", #1056-10
$85.00–95.00

Mark: Roseville in relief
Colors: Yellow/brown; Green/brown; Gray/wine

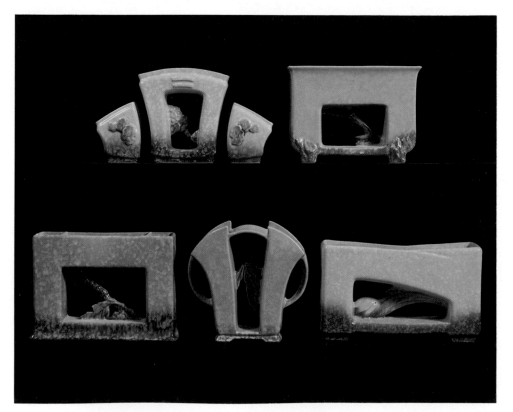

MING TREE, 1949

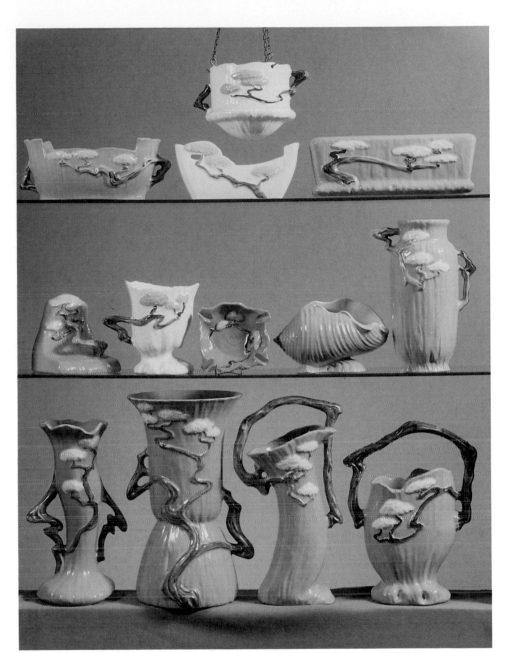

ROW 1:

Hanging Basket, 6", U.S.A.	*$225.00–250.00*
Bowl, 4" x 11½", #526–9	*$95.00–110.00*
Planter, 4" x 8½"	*$95.00–110.00*
Window Box, 4" x 11", #569–10	*$125.00–150.00*

ROW 2:

Bookend, 5½", #559	*$95.00–115.00*
Vase, 6½", #572–6	*$110.00–135.00*
Ashtray, 6", #599	*$75.00–85.00*
Conch Shell, 8½", #563	*$90.00–110.00*
Vase, 10½", #583–10	*$175.00–200.00*

ROW 3:

Vase, 12½", #584–12	*$225.00–250.00*
Vase, 14½", #585–14	*$400.00–450.00*
Basket, 14½", #510–14	*$275.00–300.00*
Basket, 13", #509–12	*$275.00–300.00*

Mark: Roseville in relief

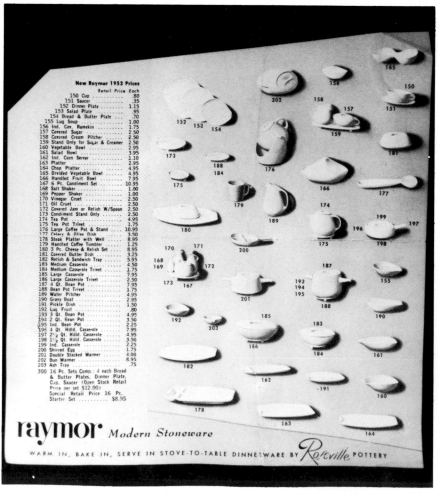

RAYMOR, 1952

ROW 1: Gravy Boat, 9½", #190..$30.00–35.00
Salad Bowl, 11½", #161...$35.00–40.00
Glass Tumblers, 4½", shown top of opposite page, ...$35.00–40.00
ROW 2: Individual Casserole,7½", #199..$40.00–45.00
Individual Corn Server, 12½", #162..$45.00–50.00
Shirred Egg, 10", #200 ....$40.00–45.00
ROW 3: Individual Covered Ramekin, 6½", #156 ....$35.00–40.00
Divided Vegetable Bowl, 13", #165..$55.00–65.00
Covered Butter, 7½", #181 ....$75.00–100.00
ROW 4: Handled Coffee Tumbler, 4", series of #s denote trial color $40.00–50.00
Condiment Set — Tray, 8½"...*$40.00–50.00*; Cruet, 5½"...*$65.00–75.00*; Mustard, 3½" $50.00–60.00
Salt and Pepper, 3½"...$30.00–35.00
Large Casserole, 13½", #185, add *$25.00* for lid $85.00–95.00
ROW 5: Vegetable, 9", #160...$30.00–40.00
Water Pitcher, 10", #189 ....$100.00–150.00
Medium Casserole, 11", #183 ....$75.00–85.00

Mark: Raymoor by Roseville, USA, in relief

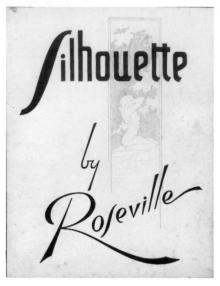

Company placard

SILHOUETTE, 1952

ROW 1: Box 4½", #740 ....$100.00–125.00
Double Planter, 5½", #757–9 ....$95.00–110.00
Ewer, 6½", #716–6 ....$75.00–85.00

ROW 2: Vase, 6", #781–6...$65.00–75.00
Vase, 8", #784–8...$85.00–95.00
Vase, 14", #789–14.......................................$200.00–250.00
Vase, 10", #787–10.......................................$450.00–500.00
Vase, 6", #780–6...$75.00–85.00

Mark: Roseville in relief

LOTUS, 1952

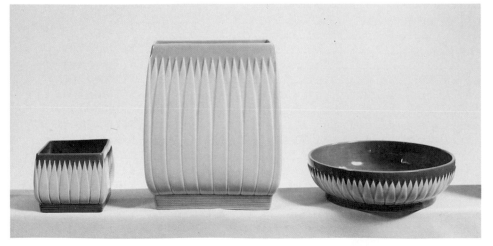

Planter, 3½" x 4", #L9–4
$90.00–100.00
Pillow Vase, 10½", #L4–10
$175.00–200.00
Bowl, 3" x 9", #L6–9
$110.00–135.00

Mark: Roseville in relief

raymor
modern artware
by Roseville
28 - 8
U.S.A.

ROW 1:
Vase, 6½", Marked as above
$150.00–$175.00
Bowl, 3" x 7", #41–6
$100.00–125.00

ROW 2:
Ashtray, Souvenir of plant tours, 3½";
yellow glaze, *$25.00–35.00*
Leaf, 10", Roseville in relief, #533–10;
undetermined line, black with frosted
rim, *$40.00–45.00*
Square dish, 4" x 2", #552 — same line as
#2, *$25.00–35.00*
Same as #1, white glaze
$25.00–35.00

ROW 3:
Wall Pocket, 10½", #711
$250.00–300.00
Vase, 12½", Roseville in relief, #593–12,
same line as R2 #2, *$125.00–150.00*
Star, 2" x 10", Roseville impressed, #713
$95.00–120.00

GLOSSY UTILITY LINE

ROW 4:
Teapot, 6½", R U.S.A., #14, light blue
glaze, *$85.00–110.00*
Cookie Jar, 10", R U.S.A., #20, green
glaze, *$150.00–175.00*
Mixing Bowl, 5½", R U.S.A., #11–8
$40.00–45.00

Left:
Bowl, 9", R U.S.A., #11–8
$55.00–65.00
Bowl, 8", R U.S.A., #10
$45.00–55.00
Bowl, 7", R U.S.A., #10–6
$35.00–40.00

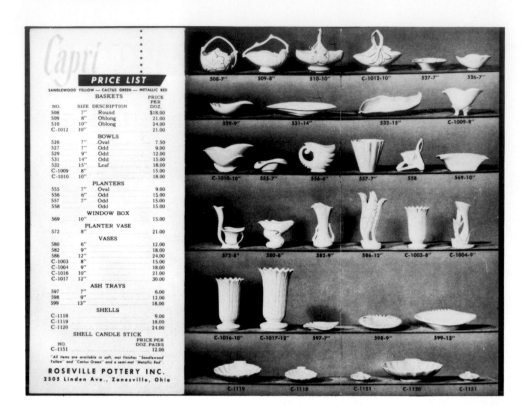
MOCK ORANGE, 1950

ROW 1:
Window Box, 8½" x 4½", #956–8
$85.00–95.00
Planter, 3½" x 9, #931–8
$100.00–125.00
Planter, 4" x 10½", #932
$100.00–125.00

ROW 2:
Vase, 8½", #973–8
$95.00–115.00
Vase, 13", #985–12
$150.00–175.00
Pillow Vase, 7", #930–8
$95.00–115.00

*Mark: Roseville U.S.A., Mock Orange,
in relief, or gold and green foil label*

156

CAPRI, late line

Above:
Basket, 9", #510–10
$125.00–150.00
Ashtray, 13", #599–3
$45.00 50.00

ROW 1:
Leaf, 16", #532–16
$25.00–35.00
Leaf, 15", #531–14
$25.00–35.00

ROW 2:
Window Box, 3" x 10", #569–10
$35.00–45.00
Planter, 5" x 10½", C–1010–10
$45.00–50.00

ROW 3:
Bowl, 9", #529–9
$20.00–25.00
Ashtray, 9", #598–9
$40.00–45.00
Bowl, 7", #527–7
$20.00–25.00

ROW 4:
Planter, 7", #558
$85.00–95.00
Shell, 13½", #C–1120
$50.00–60.00
Vase, 9", #582–9
$50.00–60.00

Mark: Roseville in relief

ROW 1:
Leaf Dish, 10½", Roseville in relief, #533–10; blue and white mottled glaze on CAPRI shape $45.00–50.00
Basket, 7", #508–7, blue and white mottled glaze, CAPRI shape $150.00–175.00

ROW 2:
CAPRI Bowl, 7", Roseville in relief, #527–7 ....$30.00–35.00
CAPRI Cornucopia, 6", Roseville in relief, #556–6 ....$85.00–95.00
Bowl, 7", Roseville impressed, #357–6, unnamed, seldom seen line...$100.00–125.00

ROW 3:
HYDE PARK Ashtray, 8½", Made in U.S.A., #1900 ....$30.00–35.00
BURMESE Candlesticks, 3", #75–B ....$45.00–50.00 pair
BURMESE Planter, 10", #908–10 ....$50.00–60.00

ROW 4:
Ashtray, 13", Roseville in relief, #599–13, black glaze, CAPRI shape...$45.00–50.00
Ashtray, 13", Roseville in relief, #204–13...$50.00–60.00

ROW 1:
Ashtray, 8½", Vernco, #1925
$25.00–30.00
Ashtray, 5½", The Hyde Park, #1915,
$30.00–35.00
Ashtray, Made in U.S.A., #1950
$30.00–35.00

ROW 2:
Tray, 8", Created Cal Art
$45.00–50.00
Planter, 4", Cal Art Creations, #1510 by
Roseville, U.S.A., *$40.00–45.00*
Section of 5-part relish, 9½" x 5½",
Roseville, #1507, *$15.00–20.00*

PASADENA

ROW 3:
Planter, 9" x 3½", Roseville, L–17,
Pasadena Planter, *$40.00–45.00*
Planter, 6½" x 5½", same mark as #1,
L–38, *$50.00–60.00*
Planter, 3½" x 10½", same mark
as #1, L–35, *$65.00–75.00*

*Raymor, Vernco, Cal Art, Hyde Park,
and Pasadena were companies for
whom Roseville produced specially
ordered wares.*

This 3-piece Kettle and Skillet set was found in its original carton. It may be found in matt black or blue and white mottled glazing.

Bowl, 2" x 5", #1797
$30.00–35.00
Skillet/Ashtray, 6½", #1799
$35.00–40.00
Pot, #1798
$30.00–35.00
Add $10.00 to each for blue.
Box *$50.00–75.00*

On reverse side the box reads: Kettle and Skillet Set, packaged by H. Bettis Co. (This Zanesville Co. later became Grief Bros.)

WALL POCKETS

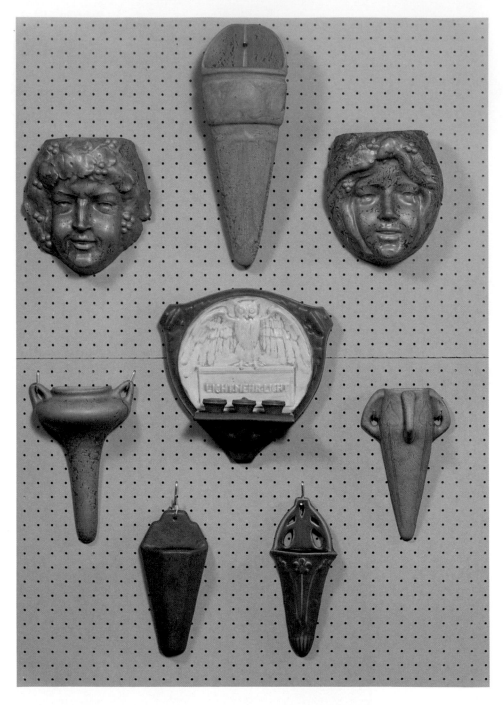

ROW 1:
CHLORON, Boy, 9½", no mark $1,000.00–1,250.00
CHLORON, Corner Vase, 17", no mark $550.00–650.00
CHLORON, Girl, 9½", no mark $1,000.00–1,250.00

ROW 2:
CHLORON, 11½", no mark $300.00–350.00
CHLORON, Sconce, 12½" x 12", no mark $1,500.00–2,000.00
CHLORON, 11", no mark $300.00–350.00

ROW 3:
ANTIQUE MATT GREEN, 10", no mark $200.00–250.00
MATT GREEN, 11", no mark $225.00–275.00

WALL POCKETS, SCONCES

ROW 1:   CHLORON Sconce, 17", no mark $1,000.00–1,500.00
                  CHLORON Sconce, 12", no mark $650.00–750.00
                  CHLORON Sconce, 17", trial glaze $1,500.00–2,000.00

ROW 2:   MATT GREEN, 15", no mark $225.00–275.00
                  CHLORON Letter Receiver, 15½", no mark $750.00–850.00
                  CHLORON Sconce, 10", no mark $600.00–700.00

ROW 3:   CHLORON/nude, 8½", no mark $750.00–850.00
                  CHLORON, 8", no mark $750.00–850.00

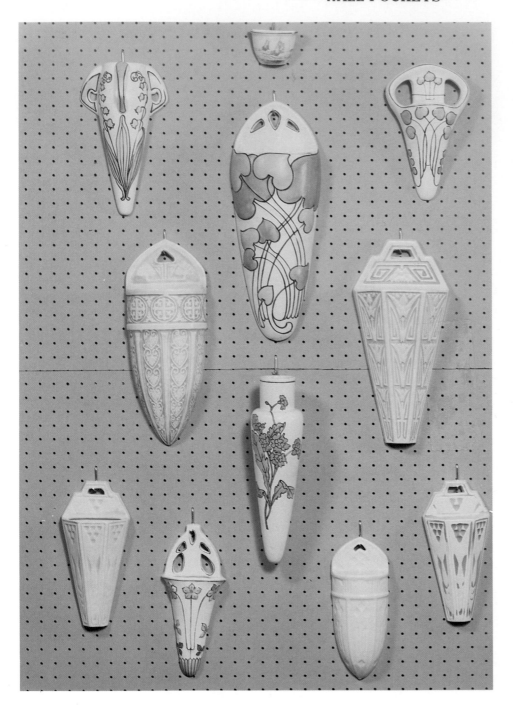

Top center:
LANDSCAPE, 2½", no mark
$300.00–350.00

ROW 1:
PERSIAN, 11", no mark
$300.00–350.00
CERAMIC DESIGN, 17", no mark
$400.00–500.00
CERAMIC DESIGN, 10", no mark
$200.00–250.00

ROW 2:
PINK TINT, 14½", no mark
$200.00–250.00
PERSIAN, 13½", no mark
$500.00–600.00
GREEN TINT, 14½", no mark
$200.00–250.00

ROW 3:
YELLOW TINT 10", no mark
$125.00–150.00
CERAMIC DESIGN, 11", no mark
$200.00–250.00
IVORY I, 10", no mark
$150.00–200.00
GREEN TINT, 10", no mark
$125.00–150.00

There is a very fine line drawn between the identification of some of these early wall pockets. Indeed in the Roseville catalogues some lines were designated "Ceramic Design" on one page — "Decorated" on another. And that term in itself was sometimes applied to the Persian line, which was in some instances called "Decorated Persian." Gold Traced…Decorated and Gold Traced — in that reference was "Decorated" again Persian? It looks the same! There are two types of decoration, you will notice — one is molded decoration, the other is not. Since we know that Persian was not molded, we associate this type with that line. To make a distinction between the two, the molded could be called Ceramic Design, without actually being incorrect.

WALL POCKETS

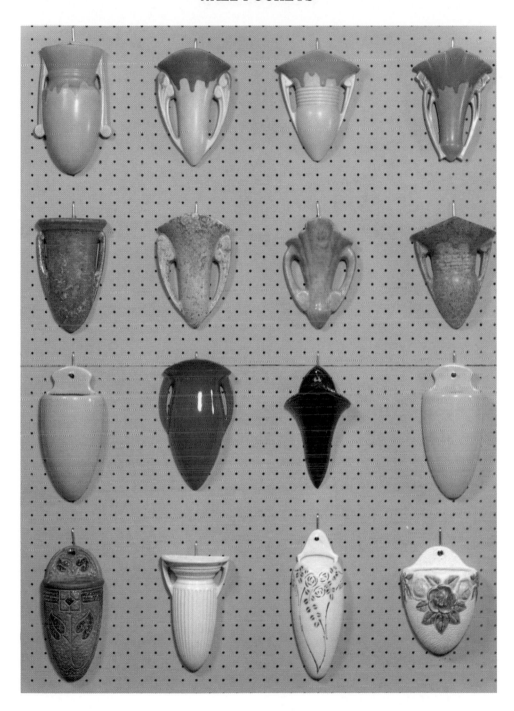

CARNELIAN I

ROW 1:

9½", Rv ink stamp $175.00–200.00

8", Rv ink stamp $175.00–200.00

8", Rv ink stamp $175.00–200.00

8", Rv ink stamp $175.00–200.00

CARNELIAN II

ROW 2:

8", black paper label $225.00–275.00

8", Rv ink stamp $225.00–275.00

8", Rv ink stamp $225.00–275.00

8", Rv ink stamp $225.00–275.00

ROW 3:

Turquoise (AZURINE, ORCHID, and TURQUOISE,
   10", no mark $150.00–175.00

ROSECRAFT BLUE, 10½", Rv ink stamp $150.00–175.00

ROSECRAFT BLACK, 9", black paper label $150.00–175.00

ROSECRAFT YELLOW, 10", Rv ink stamp $150.00–175.00

ROW 4:

MOSTIQUE, 9½", no mark..............................$225.00–250.00

VOLPATO, 8½", no mark.................................$400.00–450.00

VELMOSS SCROLL, 11", no mark...................$225.00–250.00

ROZANE 1917, 7½", Roseville Rozane Pottery,
   black ink stamp..$175.00–200.00

WALL POCKETS

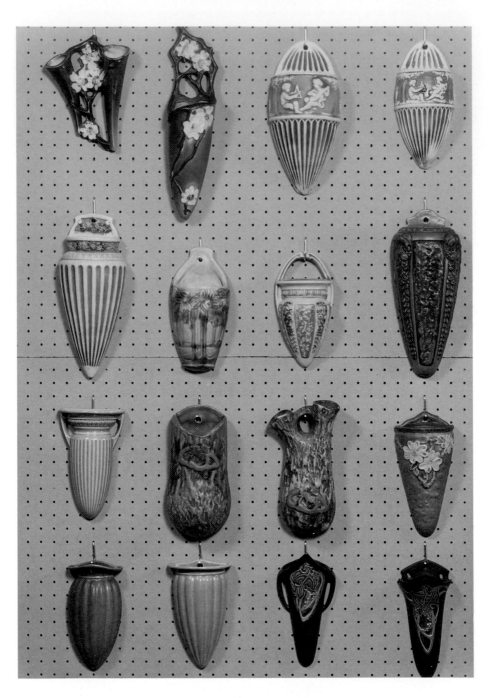

ROW 1:
DOGWOOD II, 9", no mark...................................$200.00–250.00
DOGWOOD II, 15", no mark.................................$450.00–500.00
DONATELLO, 11½", Donatello impressed seal...$125.00–150.00
DONATELLO, 9", no mark....................................$100.00–125.00

ROW 2:
CORINTHIAN, 12", no mark................................$150.00–200.00
VISTA, 9½", no mark $400.00–450.00
Ivory FLORENTINE, 8½", Roseville impressed,
   #1238 ....$150.00–175.00
FLORENTINE, 12½", Rv ink stamp $150.00–175.00

ROW 3:
SAVONA, 8", black paper label $400.00–450.00
IMPERIAL I, 10", no mark $150.00–175.00
IMPERIAL I, 10", no mark $150.00–175.00
DOGWOOD I, 9½", Rv ink stamp $150.00–175.00

ROW 4:
LOMBARDY, 8", black paper label, matt glaze $250.00–300.00
LOMBARDY, 8", black paper label, glossy glaze...$250.00–300.00
ROSECRAFT VINTAGE, 9", Rv ink stamp $175.00–200.00
ROSECRAFT VINTAGE, 9", Rv ink stamp $175.00–200.00

WALL POCKETS

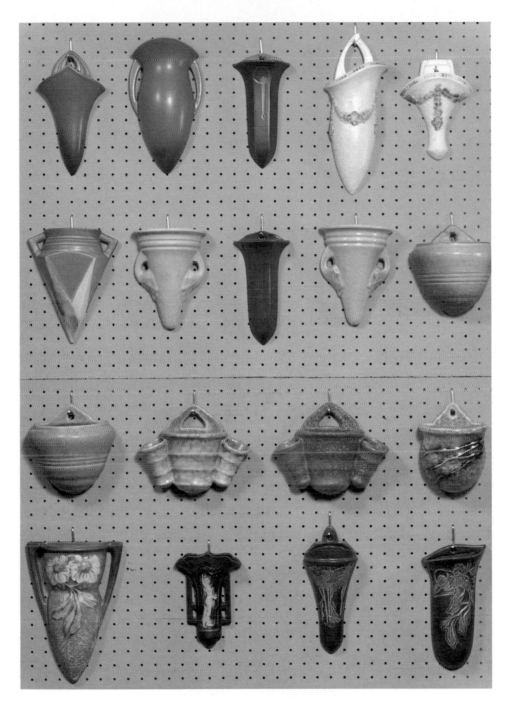

ROW 1:

FLORANE, 9", Rv ink stamp $125.00–150.00
FLORANE, 10½", Rv ink stamp..........................$150.00–175.00
ROSECRAFT HEXAGON, 8½", Rv ink stamp $350.00–400.00
LA ROSE, 12", Rv ink stamp...............................$200.00–250.00
LA ROSE, 7½", Rv ink stamp $125.00–150.00

ROW 2:

FUTURA, 8", no mark...$400.00–450.00
TUSCANY, 7", blue glaze, no mark $200.00–225.00
ROSECRAFT HEXAGON, 8½", Rv ink stamp,
    note blue glaze $400.00–450.00
TUSCANY, 7", no mark...$225.00–250.00
EARLAM, 6½", black paper label $300.00–350.00

ROW 3:

IMPERIAL II, 6½", no mark $300.00–350.00
IMPERIAL II, 6½", trial glaze $325.00–350.00
IMPERIAL II, 6½", no mark $350.00–400.00
IMPERIAL II, 6½", black paper label...................$350.00–400.00

ROW 4:

DAHLROSE, 10", no mark....................................$175.00–200.00
PANEL, 7", Rv ink stamp $500.00–600.00
PANEL, 9", Rv ink stamp $175.00–200.00
PANEL, 9", Rv ink stamp $200.00–225.00

(Panel's proper name was shown in company records as
Rosecraft Panel.)

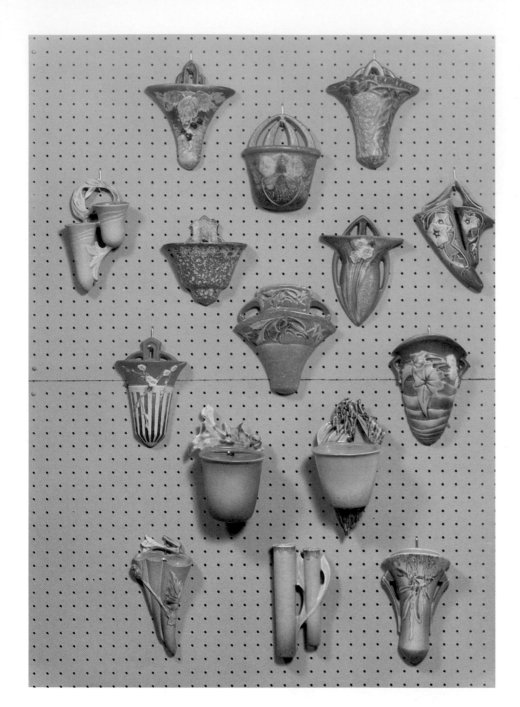

WALL POCKETS

ROW 1:
BLACKBERRY, 8½", no mark
$700.00–800.00
SUNFLOWER, 7½", no mark
$600.00–700.00
WISTERIA, 8", no mark
$750.00–850.00

ROW 2:
VELMOSS, 8½", no mark
$550.00–600.00
FERELLA, 6½", no mark
$800.00–900.00
BANEDA, 8", silver paper label
$1,250.00–1,500.00
JONQUIL, 8½", no mark
$450.00–500.00
MORNING GLORY, 8½", no mark
$650.00–700.00

ROW 3:
CHERRY BLOSSOM, 8", silver
paper label, *$500.00–600.00*
THORN APPLE, 8½", no mark
$650.00–700.00
MOSS, 10", Roseville impressed,
#1279, *$650.00–700.00*
LUFFA, 8½", no mark
$500.00–550.00

ROW 4:
THORN APPLE, 8", Roseville
impressed, #1280–8
$400.00–450.00
ORIAN, 8", no mark
$400.00–450.00
MOSS, 8", Roseville impressed,
#1278–8, *$350.00–400.00*

ROYAL CAPRI, late line

Opposite page, bottom left:
Leaf, 2" x 10½", #533–10
$200.00–225.00
Vase, 9", #583–9
$250.00–275.00

Bottom right:
Wall Pocket, 5", #1–1
$300.00–400.00

Mark: Roseville in relief

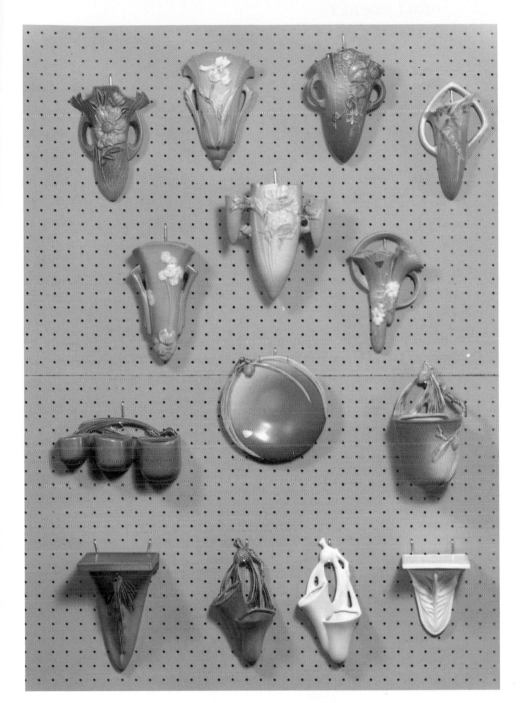

WALL POCKETS

ROW 1:
PEONY, 8", Roseville in relief, #1293–8, *$150.00–200.00*
IRIS, 8", Roseville impressed, #1284–8, *$300.00–350.00*
FUCHSIA, 8½", Roseville impressed, #128–8, *$400.00–450.00*
BLEEDING HEART, 8½", Roseville in relief, #1287–8, *$300.00–350.00*

ROW 2:
PRIMROSE, 8½", Roseville impressed, #177–8, *$400.00–450.00*
POPPY, 8½", Roseville impressed, #1281, *$450.00–500.00*
COSMOS, 8½", silver paper label, #1286–8, *$300.00–350.00*

ROW 3:
PINECONE, 8½", Roseville in relief, #466, brown, *$350.00–400.00;* blue, *$500.00–550.00;* green, *$275.00–325.00*
PINECONE Plate, 7½", silver paper label, *$300.00–350.00*
PINECONE, 9", Roseville impressed, #1283, *$700.00–750.00*

ROW 4:
PINECONE Wall Shelf, Roseville in relief, #1, *$400.00–450.00*
PINECONE, 8½", Roseville impressed, #1273–8 *$300.00–350.00*
IVORY II, 8½", same as #2 *$150.00–175.00*
IVORY II Shelf, 5½", Roseville impressed, #8, *$125.00–150.00*

ROYAL CAPRI, late line

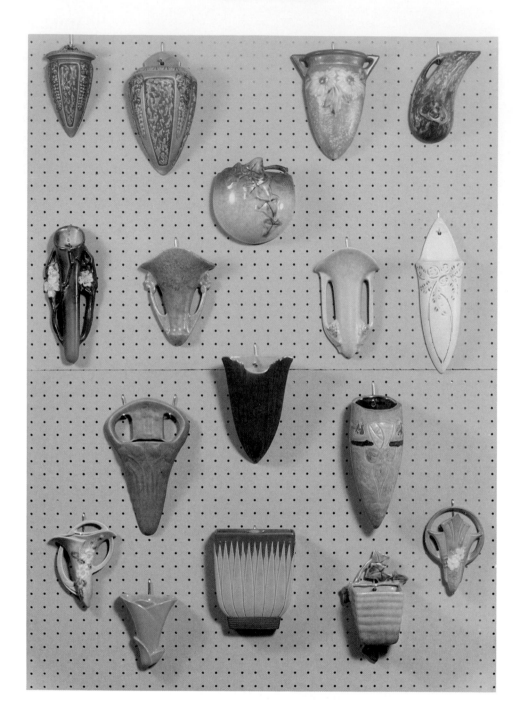

ROW 1:
FLORENTINE, 7", Rv ink stamp $125.00–150.00
FLORENTINE, 9½", no mark.......................$125.00–175.00
DAHLROSE, 9", black paper label $125.00–175.00
IMPERIAL I, 8", no mark..............................$175.00–200.00

ROW 2:
WINCRAFT, 5", Roseville in relief,
   #267–5 ....$150.00–175.00

ROW 3:
DOGWOOD II, 10", Rv ink stamp.................$250.00–300.00
CARNELIAN II, 7", Rv ink stamp $225.00–275.00
TUSCANY, 8", black paper label....................$150.00–175.00
VELMOSS SCROLL, 11½", no mark............$250.00–300.00

ROW 4:
CHLORON, 10½", no mark $225.00–250.00
MAYFAIR, 8", corner pocket, Roseville in relief,
   #1014–8 ....$125.00–150.00
MOSTIQUE, 10½", no mark $150.00–175.00

ROW 5:
WHITE ROSE, 6½", Roseville in relief,
   #1288–6 ....$175.00–200.00
CAPRI trial glaze, 5", Roseville in relief, #1013–5, with
   series of code numbers denoting
   trial glaze..$250.00–300.00
LOTUS, 7½", Lotus in relief, L8–7 ....$200.00–250.00
WINCRAFT, 8½", Roseville in relief, #266–4 .$175.00–200.00
COSMOS, 6½", Roseville in relief, #1285 ....$175.00–200.00

ROW 1:
GARDENIA, 9½", #666–8 ....$200.00–225.00
FOXGLOVE, 8", #1292–8........................$300.00–350.00
COLUMBINE, 8½", #1290–8 ....$300.00–350.00
FREESIA, 8½", #1296–8........................$125.00–150.00

ROW 2:
APPLE BLOSSOM, 8½", #366–8 ....$175.00–200.00
ZEPHYR LILY, 8", #1297–8, this example is marked
   under the glaze with the # series denoting trial,
   and was the prototype original $150.00–200.00
MAGNOLIA, 8½", #1294 ....$200.00–225.00
BITTERSWEET, 7½", #866–7.................$150.00–200.00

ROW 3:
WHITE ROSE, 8½", #1289–8................$275.00–325.00
SNOWBERRY, 8", #1WP–8 ....$150.00–175.00
CLEMATIS, 8½", #1295–8.....................$150.00–175.00
BUSHBERRY, 8", #1291–8.....................$250.00–300.00
   blue...$275.00–325.00

ROW 4:
SILHOUETTE, 8", #766–8 ....$150.00–175.00
BURMESE, 7½", #72–B, blue glaze $200.00–250.00
BURMESE, 7½", #82–B, white glaze $200.00–250.00
MING TREE, 8½" #566–8.....................$250.00–300.00
Mark: Roseville in relief

EXPERIMENTALS

ROW 1: Freesia design, 9", blue background, yellow flowers *$1,000.00–1,250.00*
Gladiola design, inscribed on back: "GLADIOLUS"; green with white flowers *$1,000.00–1,250.00*
Lupines design, inscribed on back: "Pure White, White and Blue, Blue and Pink" *$1,000.00–1,250.00*

ROW 2: Black Eyed Susan: "yellow petals, center disk brown," blue background *$1,000.00–1,250.00*
Orchid, dark green background, white orchids *$1,000.00–1,250.00*
Blackberry, artist signed FAB, shaded green background *$1,000.00–1,250.00*

ROW 3: White Rose design, pink to blue with yellow rose *$1,000.00–1,250.00*
Bittersweet; incised on back: "Open shells, yellow orange, berries red, leaves green," background is blue *$1,000.00–1,250.00*
Geranium, tan to green with pink flowers *$1,000.00–1,250.00*

ROW 4: Arrowhead design, inscription: "Flowers — white, leaves — green, flower centers — orange, buds — yellow green with
white edges," background in blue *$1,000.00–1,250.00*
Arrowhead design, inscription: "Flowers — white, leaves — green," pink to blue background *$1,000.00–1,250.00*
Larkspur design, inscription: "White, pink, blue, lavender, salmon (centers yellow)," background is blue *$1,000.00–1,250.00*

EXPERIMENTALS

ROW 1:
Pinecone design, 6"
$550.00–650.00
Pinecone design, 8"
$700.00–800.00
Vase, 5"
$300.00–350.00

ROW 2:
Nude, 10", Panel type
$1,250.00–1,500.00
Nude, 10"
$1,250.00–1,500.00
Nude, 10"
$1,250.00–1,500.00

ROW 3:
Nude, 12½"
$1,250.00–1,500.00
Pinecone design, 20½"
1,500.00–1,750.00
Dogwood design, 16½",
decorated over Vista blank
$1,000.00–1,250.00

TRIALS

"Serra," 6"
$175.00–225.00
Pinecone, 9", notation: "Bought
at Chicago World's Fair, 1932"
$500.00–600.00
Vase, 9"
$500.00–600.00
Mock Orange, 8", Roseville in
relief, #974–8
$200.00–250.00
Decorated Imperial II, 5"
$250.00–300.00

EXPERIMENTALS

ROW 1:
Primrose design, 10", blue and tan with white flowers and green leaves.
Sweet Syrinca or Mock Orange, 8½"; blue with white blossoms, yellow centers.
Vase, 8", green and tan with white blossoms, green leaves.
Vase, 10", tan with white blossoms, green leaves.
$800.00–900.00 each

ROW 2:
Gladiola design, 9½", soft tan into light blue, pale yellow flowers
$700.00–800.00
Bittersweet Vase, 13", shown in greenware, notation on base: Fruit, yellow, orange; Leaves rich green; white, yellow centers, *$500.00–600.00*
Arrowhead design, 13", also in greenware, same colors indicated on base
$500.00–600.00
Freesia design, 8½", tan to pale blue, light yellow flower
$700.00–800.00

TRIAL GLAZES

ROW 1:
8" Plates, each with series of numbers representing color codes
$200.00–250.00, each

ROW 2:
Planter, 3", Roseville in relief, #s indicate trial glaze, *$100.00–150.00*
MING TREE, 8", in salmon pink with greenery, *$200.00–300.00*
Window Box, 3½" x 10", tan to blue
$125.00–175.00

ROW 3:
LAUREL, 8", ice blue to darker blue at base, *$500.00–600.00*
WILD ROSE Experimental, 10", pink to blue, white flowers, *$500.00–600.00*
Vase, 8½", blue mottled with brown contrast, *$400.00–475.00*
MODERNE, 8", #796-8, tan to green
$175.00–250.00

TRIALS, EXPERIMENTALS

ROW 1: (Trials)
Tulip Vase, 6", Roseville in relief,
#1001–6, *$250.00–300.00*
Savona, 6"
$250.00–300.00
Baneda, 6"
$450.00–500.00
"New Colors" incised on base, 7",
Rozane RPCo die stamp
$150.00–200.00
Cherry Blossom Bowl, 4"
$400.00–450.00

ROW 2:
Morning Glory, 8", with textured
modeling on background, experimental, *$800.00–1,000.00*
Morning Glory, in yellow and ivory,
trial glaze, *$800.00–900.00*
Morning Glory; in brown, gold, and
pink; trial glaze; *$800.00–1,000.00*

ROW 3: (Experimentals)
Cherry Blossom, 7"
$850.00–950.00
Cosmos over Teasel blank, 8",
Roseville in relief, #884
$700.00–800.00
Freesia design, 7"
$600.00–650.00
Stylized Honeysuckle, 6½"
$400.00–450.00

ROW 4: (Experimentals)
Floral design, 8"
$650.00–750.00
Wild Grape design, 9½"
1,000.00–1,250.00
Cherry Blossom design, 7"
600.00–700.00

These trial glaze plates, left and
right, measure 9½", and were from
George Krause's estate. The Blackberry
plate in the center ia an experimental
and is dated 11/19/63. A company letter
in the Roseville files discusses the possi-
bility of using some of the more popular
older patterns as a basis for a dinner-
ware line...Blackberry was specifically
suggested. ....*$250.00–450.00 ea.*

UMBRELLA STANDS

#727 BLENDED, 20", no mark
$250.00–350.00
EARLAM, 20", silver paper label, #741
$500.00–600.00
#609 BLENDED, 20", no mark
$275.00–350.00

LAMPS

Base, 11½", marked with series of #s
$225.00–325.00
IMPERIAL II, 5", black paper label
$300.00–400.00
Base, 12", no mark
$400.00–450.00
Base, 8½", no mark
$250.00–300.00

LAMPS

ROW 1:
Base, 8", small black paper label, #34–4
$350.00–400.00
Base, 8", small black paper label, #F39–4
$350.00–400.00

ROW 2:
Base, 7", small black paper label
$225.00–275.00
Base, 10", silver paper label, #F84–R7
$450.00–550.00
Base, 7½", no mark
$450.00–500.00

ROW 3:
Base, 8½", no mark
$150.00–200.00
Base, 10½", no mark
$450.00–550.00
Base, 5½", small silver paper label
$175.00–250.00

RADIATOR COVER

One of a set of radiator covers from the home of Russell T. Young, son of the founder of the Roseville Pottery, George Young. The design was by Frank Ferrell, George Krause made the tile. NPA.

UMBRELLA STANDS

BLENDED Basketweave, 21", marked
with small paper label, *$250.00–350.00*

#701 BLENDED, 22", no mark,
$250.00–325.00
#734 BLENDED, 21", marked with large
paper label, *$200.00–225.00*

#132 BLENDED, 21½"
$300.00–400.00
BLENDED Stork, 19", #705
$300.00–375.00
#719 BLENDED, 22"
$300.00–400.00

BLENDED, 29½", #126
$400.00–500.00
MATT GREEN, 36", no mark
$2,000.00–2,500.00
DECORATED CREAMWARE, 29",
no mark, *$600.00–750.00*

IVORY FLORENTINE, 29",
no mark, *$600.00–700.00*
IVORY CAMEO, 34", Jard, #439
$1,000.00–1,250.00
ROZANE 1917, 28½", no mark
$450.00–550.00

Above:
DECORATE LANDSCAPE, 43"
$3,000.00–4,000.00
Umbrella Stand with sgraffito and
squeezebag, 22"
$1,750.00–2,250.00
DECORATED LANDSCAPE, 44"
$3,000.00–4,000.00

Right:
BLENDED Iris, 31", #451
$500.00–600.00
#441 BLENDED, 38"
$600.00–800.00
#414 BLENDED, 28"
$400.00–600.00

Early CERAMIC, 49", no mark
$1,500.00–1,700.00
FLEUR DE LIS, 20½", Jard, #412
$400.00–450.00

Gold and Silver Decorated, 22½",
no mark
$900.00–1,200.00
DECORATED MATT, 20", #724,
(artist's cipher unknown)
$2,500.00–3,000.00
Gold and Silver Decorated, 21½",
no mark
$900.00–1,100.00

UMBRELLA STANDS

NORMANDY, 20", no mark
$600.00–700.00
TOURIST, 22½", no mark
$3,000.00–3,500.00
CORINTHIAN, 20", Rv ink stamp
$400.00–500.00

JARDINIERES AND PEDESTALS

DONATELLO, 34", no mark
$1,000.00–1,250.00
ROSECRAFT VINTAGE, 30½",
Rv ink stamp
$850.00–1,000.00
CORINTHIAN, 30½", Rv ink stamp
$500.00–600.00

IVORY II, Sand Jar, 14½", no mark
$250.00–300.00
IVORY FLORENTINE Urn, 16½",
Roseville in relief, #297
$325.00–400.00
IVORY FLORENTINE Umbrella,
18½", Roseville in relief, #298
$250.00–350.00
NORMANDY Sand Jar, 14", no mark
$350.00–400.00

JARDINIERES AND PEDESTALS

DECORATED CREAMWARE with
Rose decal, 26", no mark
$750.00–850.00
ROZANE, 28", Rozane RPCo die
stamp, #516 on pedestal
$900.00–1,000.00
FLORENTINE, 25", no mark
$675.00–775.00
WISTERIA, 24½", no mark
$1,500.00–2,000.00
blue, *2,500.00–3,000.00*

ROZANE FLOOR VASES

Vase, 25", Rozane RPCo die stamp,
#850–3 (W Myers '02)
$1,500.00–2,000.00
Vase, 29½", Rozane Ware seal,
(Mitchell)
$3,000.00–3,500.00
Vase, 20", small die stamp,
#632 (L McGrath)
$1,500.00–2,000.00

JARDINIERES AND PEDESTALS

DONATELLO, 23½", no mark
$500.00–600.00
ARTCRAFT, 24½", no mark
$750.00–950.00
CHERRY BLOSSOM, 25½", no mark
$2,000.00–2,500.00
CORINTHIAN, 24", Rv ink stamp
$450.00–550.00

ARTCRAFT, 28", no mark
$900.00–1,000.00
BLACKBERRY, 28", no mark
$2,900.00–3,200.00
DAHLROSE, 30½", no mark
$800.00–900.00

JARDINIERES AND PEDESTALS

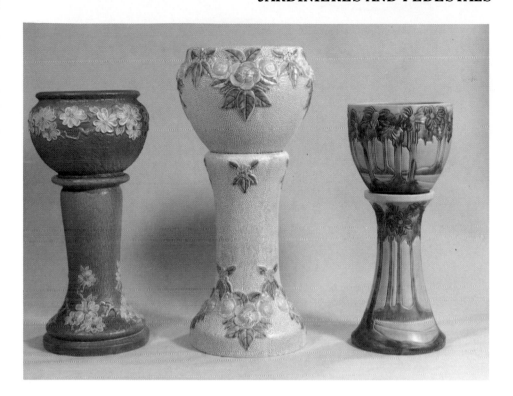

DOGWOOD I, 30",
small Rv ink stamp
$650.00–750.00
ROZANE 1917, 35",
Rozane Pottery ink stamp
$450.00–600.00
FOREST, 28", no mark
$1,250.00–1,500.00

JONQUIL, 29", no mark
$1,250.00–1,600.00
NORMANDY, 28", Rv ink stamp
$800.00–900.00
SUNFLOWER, 29", no mark
$2,000.00–3,000.00

#720 MATT GREEN Umbrella Stand, 23", no mark................................$350.00–450.00
PEONY Jardiniere & Pedestal, 30", Roseville in relief, #661 on jard. $650.00–750.00
BLENDED Mostique Jardiniere and Pedestal, 27½", no mark...............$450.00–500.00

BIRDBATH/PLANTER, 30", overall height; 18½" across;
pot, 7½"; Roseville in relief, #296 on birdbath, #295 on pot
$300.00–400.00

FOXGLOVE Jardiniere and Pedestal, 30½", Roseville in relief,
#659 on jard., *$800.00–1,000.00*
ROSECRAFT BLENDED, 28", no mark
$750.00–850.00

SNOWBERRY, 25", Roseville in relief,
#1P8 U.S.A. on ped; #1J8 on jard.
$550.00–650.00
LUFFA, 24½", no mark
1,000.00–1,250.00
LA ROSE, 24½", Rv ink stamp
$750.00–850.00
ZEPHYR LILY, 25", Roseville in relief,
#671–8, *$550.00–650.00*

EARLAM Floor Vase, 12⅛", silver
paper label, *$500.00–600.00*
CARNELIAN I, Floor Vase, 18½", Rv
ink stamp, *$450.00–500.00*
MING TREE Floor Vase, 15½",
Roseville in relief, #586–15
$550.00–650.00
#708 BLENDED Umbrella Stand,
19½", no mark, *$350.00–450.00*
FLORANE, Late Line Sand Jar, 12",
R in relief, #52–12
$125.00–150.00

BUSHBERRY Umbrella Stand, 20½",
Roseville in relief, #779–20
$600.00–700.00
SUNFLOWER, 20½", small black
paper label
$2,000.00–2,500.00
DOGWOOD II, 19½", no mark
$350.00–450.00

Autumn Jars

Donatello

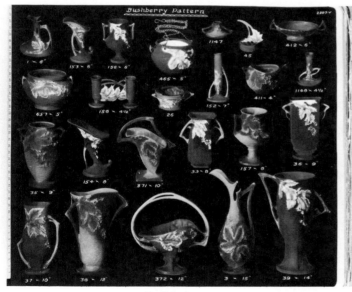

Bushberry

Donatello

Cosmos

Ferella

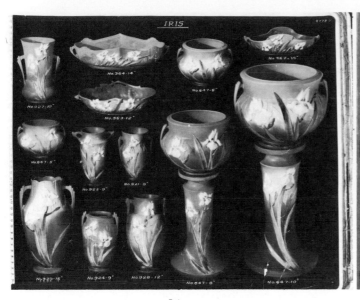

Iris

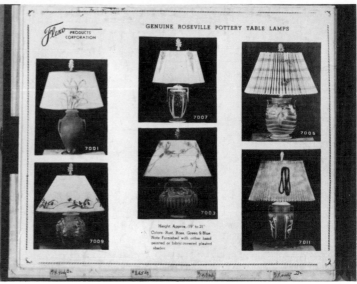

Lamps

Ixia

Lamps

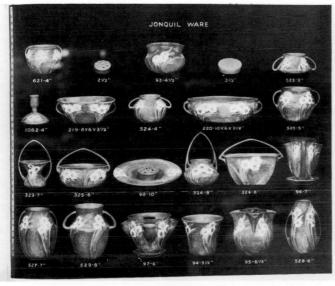

Jonquil

Laurel

Montacello

Persian

Moss

Pinecone

Mostique

Mostique

Poppy

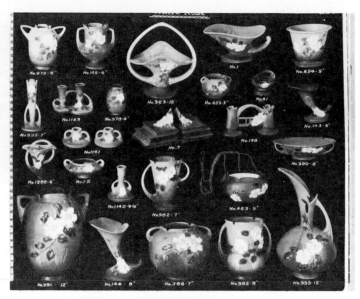

White Rose

Poppy

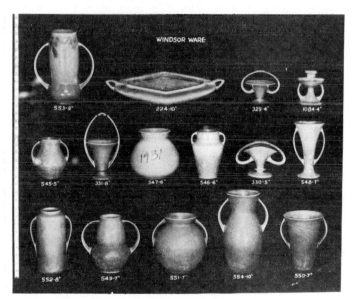

Windsor Ware

Thorn Apple

Thorn Apple

BIBLIOGRAPHY

Alexander, Donald E; ROSEVILLE POTTERY FOR COLLECTORS; published by the author, 1970

Hall, Foster and Gladys; HALLS PRICING FORMULAS; published by the authors, continually updated

Ohio Historical Society; Roseville catalogues from their files

PAULEO POTTERY, Roseville Company booklet, 1914

Schneider, Norris; BLUE AVENUE MAN AND WIFE FOREMOST AUTHORI-TIES ON ROSEVILLE POTTERY; The Times Recorder, March 31, 1968

THE STORY OF ROZANE; Roseville Pottery Company booklet

1905 ROZANE WARE CATALOGUE, Roseville Company

1906 ROZANE WARE CATALOGUE, Roseville Company

1916 PRICE LISTING, Roseville Company

INDEX

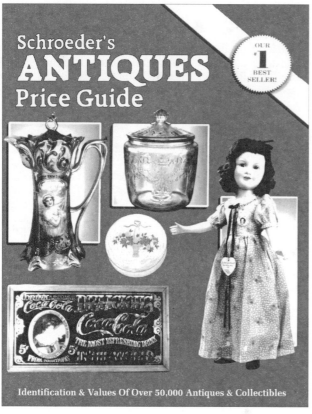